Southern Cooking

Southern Cooking

Ruthann Carter

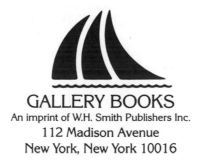

GALLERY BOOKS

An imprint of W.H. Smith Publishers Inc.

112 Madison Avenue

New York, New York 10016

ISBN: 0–8317–7931–4

Published in the United States by
Gallery Books
An Imprint of W.H. Smith Publishers, Inc.
112 Madison Avenue
New York, New York 10016

This book was designed and produced by
Footnote Productions Ltd.
6 Blundell Street
London N7 9BH

Color origination by Hong Kong Scanner Craft, Ltd.
Printed by Lee Fung Asco Printers, Ltd.

Contents

🌿 Appetizers 🌿

One of the biggest problems I have with Sunday dinners or large dinner parties has nothing to do with cooking. It's getting everybody to the table at the same time. Seems there's always a football game that goes on forever, or everyone's out back throwing horseshoes, or something. And there I am, with everything piping hot and cooked just right, staring at all those empty chairs. What do I do? I just send whoever's been helping me in the kitchen out to where everybody is to announce "Mama says the crab cakes are just getting too cold to eat, so she's taking them off the table." And not more than a minute later we're all sitting round the table passing the tartar sauce and lemon wedges.

I guarantee that after you've served these appetizers to your family and friends, you won't have a lick of trouble getting everyone to the table on time.

All these recipes can be used for cocktail parties, buffets or just a late-night snack. They're so easy to prepare that it won't matter whether you've got a whole week to set up for a large party, or just an hour or two when folks just come by. Just make sure you've got lots of toothpicks, napkins, and time to take in all the compliments.

🌿 Avocado Appetizer

3 ripe avocados
1 cup chopped seedless red grapes
1 cup white raisins or currants
½ cup honey
1 cup warm water
½ teaspoon ground nutmeg
⅛ teaspoon ground ginger
dry Madeira wine, chilled

Halve the avocados lengthwise and remove the pits. Put each avocado half in a small dessert bowl.

Put the grapes, raisins or currants, honey, water, nutmeg, and ginger in a saucepan. Simmer over very low heat, stirring occasionally, until the honey is well blended. Pour the mixture into a bowl and let cool at room temperature for 30 minutes.

Fill each avocado half with the fruit and honey mixture. Drizzle a few spoonfuls of the dry Madeira over each and serve.

serves 6

🌿 Charleston Crab Cakes

2 eggs
1 pound fresh crabmeat, picked and flaked
1 small white onion, diced
¼ teaspoon salt
½ teaspoon white pepper
2 tablespoons fine, seasoned breadcrumbs
butter or light vegetable oil for frying

In a mixing bowl beat the eggs until frothy. Mix in the crabmeat, diced onion, salt, pepper and breadcrumbs. Blend well.

In a skillet, put enough butter or oil to cover the bottom of the skillet to a depth of about ¼ inch. Heat slowly. When hot, spoon out the crab mixture in cakes about 2 or 3 inches across and place in the hot butter or oil. When the crab cakes are golden brown on one side, turn them, using two spoons and being very careful not to break the cakes. Fry all the crab mixture, making only a few cakes at a time, adding more butter or oil as needed. When all the cakes have cooled, squeeze a little lemon juice over each. Serve with tartar sauce.

serves 8

🦐 Deep-Fried Ham Fritters

1 pound baked Virginia ham
½ cup unsweetened crushed pineapple, drained
¾ cup white flour
1 teaspoon baking powder
¼ cup light cream
¼ cup cold water
1 teaspoon Angostura or Peychand's bitters
1 teaspoon sherry
2 eggs
oil for deep frying

Mince or grind the ham until it is like coarse meal. Mix the pineapple together with the ham in a bowl.

Sift the flour and baking powder together in a mixing bowl. Add the cream, water, bitters, sherry and eggs and beat until the mixture is smooth. Fold in the ham and pineapple mixture and mix together with a wooden spoon until well blended.

Set the bowl in the freezer for about 15 minutes.

Heat the oil in a deep fryer until it is no hotter than 350°F.

Drop large spoonfuls of the fritter mixture, using a spatula to scrape the spoonfuls into the deep-fryer. Cook until the fritters are golden brown. Drain on paper towels and serve hot with applesauce or spicy mustard.

serves 15

🦐 Gulf Crab Soufflés

2 tablespoons butter
2 tablespoons flour
½ teaspoon salt
⅛ teaspoon black pepper
1 cup milk
2 eggs, separated
1 pound fresh crabmeat, picked and flaked
1 cup heavy cream, whipped

Preheat the oven to 350°.

In a saucepan, melt the butter and add the flour, salt, and pepper. Blend well. Slowly add the milk, stirring constantly. Cook until the mixture begins to thicken. Remove from heat.

In a separate bowl, add 1 tablespoon of the hot milk mixture to the egg yolks; stir the yolks into the hot milk mixture. Add the crabmeat and fold in the whipped cream.

In another bowl beat the egg whites until they are stiff but not dry. Fold the egg whites into the crabmeat mixture.

Place the mixture into 6 buttered individual soufflé or casserole dishes. Set the dishes in a large pan of water. The water should come halfway up the sides of the dishes.

Bake for 40 minutes or until firm. Serve *immediately.*

serves 6

🎝 Creole Canapés

1 cup boiled ham, minced
1 tablespoon butter
1 medium onion, finely chopped
1 garlic clove, finely chopped
1 medium-sized tomato, seeded and chopped
1 green pepper, finely chopped
salt to taste
black pepper to taste
cayenne pepper to taste
6 slices buttered toast, cut into strips
¼ cup freshly grated Parmesan cheese

Melt the butter in a skillet. Add the ham, onion and garlic and sauté for 3 minutes. Add the green pepper and tomato. Continue cooking. Season to taste with salt, pepper, and cayenne pepper. Cook the mixture until it is dry and thick, about 35 minutes.

Preheat the oven to 375°.

When ready to serve, place the spread on strips of buttered toast and sprinkle with cheese. Put the strips on a baking sheet and bake for 5 to 7 minutes. Serve hot.

serves 6

🎝 Deep-Fried Hominy Balls

2 cups water
½ teaspoon salt
½ cup quick-cooking hominy grits
1 cup grated sharp Cheddar cheese
¼ teaspoon cayenne pepper
¼ teaspoon grated nutmeg
2 eggs
1½ teaspoons olive oil
1½ cups unflavored breadcrumbs
oil for frying

In a saucepan, bring the water and salt to a boil. Slowly add the grits. Stir well. Bring the mixture back to a boil and reduce the heat. Cook the grits for 3 to 5 minutes, stirring occasionally. Remove from heat and chill.

Place the chilled grits in a bowl and mash them well with a fork. Stir in the grated cheese, cayenne, nutmeg and pepper. Shape mixture into about 40 1-inch balls. (A melon baller is useful for this.)

In a small bowl beat together the eggs and olive oil. Dip the balls in the egg mixture and then in the breadcrumbs.

Heat the oil to 375° in a deep skillet. Fry the balls in batches until they are golden brown, about 2 minutes. Drain on paper towels and serve.

serves 6 to 8

🎝 Party Pecans

2 tablespoons peanut oil
½ cup Worcestershire sauce
1 tablespoon mild barbecue sauce
¼ teaspoon Tabasco sauce
4 cups pecan halves
salt to taste
black pepper to taste

Pour the peanut oil, Worcestershire sauce, barbecue sauce and Tabasco sauce into a mixing bowl and stir. Stir in the pecans.

Preheat the oven to 300°.

Line a baking pan with aluminum foil and spread the pecans and sauce evenly on it. Bake for 30 minutes stirring every 7 minutes. drain the roasted pecans on brown paper. Season with salt and pepper to taste.

makes 4 cups

🦐 Latin Quarter Green Tomatoes

4 large green tomatoes
¼ teaspoon salt
¼ teaspoon cayenne pepper
¼ teaspoon dried basil
1 cup cornmeal
4 bacon strips
lettuce leaves

Cut the tomatoes into quarters (if the tomatoes are very large, cut them into eighths). Sprinkle the salt, cayenne, and basil over all sides of the cut tomatoes. Spread the cornmeal on a plate.

Cut the bacon strips into bite-sized pieces and cook them in a skillet until the pieces become transparant and the skillet has begun to fill with drippings. Remove and reserve the half-cooked bacon pieces.

Dredge the tomato wedges in the cornmeal, coating both sides, and fry them in the bacon drippings over medium heat. When all the tomato wedges are in the skillet, add the reserved bacon pieces and fry, turning the tomatoes to cook on both sides, until the bacon is done and the tomatoes are tender and browned.

Serve hot on a bed of lettuce leaves.

serves **6**

🦐 Shrimp Fritters

1 cup flour
1 teaspoon baking powder
½ teaspoon salt
¼ teaspoon black pepper
2 eggs, beaten
½ cup milk
⅓ cup finely chopped onion
½ teaspoon Tabasco sauce
1 pound uncooked shrimp, peeled, deveined and coarsely chopped
oil for deep frying

In a mixing bowl combine the flour, baking powder, salt and pepper. Stir in the eggs and enough of the milk to make a thick batter. Add the onion, Tabasco sauce, and shrimp. Mix until shrimp pieces are well coated.

Heat the oil to 375° in a deep skillet. Drop the batter by teaspoons into the oil. Fry until golden brown, in batches, about 2 minutes.

Serve hot with cocktail sauce or tartar sauce.

serves **6**

🦐 Shreveport Shrimp

2 pounds cooked shrimp, peeled and deveined
¾ cup white wine or dry vermouth
¼ teaspoon black pepper
⅛ teaspoon cayenne pepper
4 tablespoons butter
1 cup unflavored breadcrumbs
2 garlic cloves, crushed
½ teaspoon salt

Preheat the oven to 350°.

Butter a 15-inch baking pan. Spread the shrimp over the bottom of the pan. Pour in the wine and sprinkle the shrimp with the pepper and cayenne. Dot the shrimp with 1 tablespoon of the butter cut into small pieces.

In a saucepan melt the remaining butter. Remove from the heat and mix in the breadcrumbs, garlic and salt. Spread the mixture evenly over the shrimp. Bake for 20 minutes. Serve hot.

serves 6

❧ Pickled Shrimp

2 pounds shrimp, in the shell
¼ cup mixed pickling spices
1 cup vegetable oil
¾ cup white vinegar
1 teaspoon salt
¼ teaspoon black pepper
2 teaspoons celery seeds
1 teaspoon Tabasco sauce
1 large onion, chopped

In a saucepan combine the unshelled shrimp and pickling spices. Add enough water to cover the shrimp completely. Cover tightly, bring to a boil, reduce the heat, and simmer for 3 to 5 minutes. Remove the saucepan from the heat and allow the shrimp to cool in the liquid. When completely cool, shell the shrimp.

In a small bowl, combine the vegetable oil, vinegar, salt, pepper, celery seeds and Tabasco sauce. Mix well.

Arrange layers of shrimp and chopped onion in a bowl. Add the oil and vinegar mixture, cover, and chill 8 hours or overnight.

serves 6 to 8

❧ Seafood Puffs

1 cup beer
8 tablespoons butter
1 cup flour
½ teaspoon salt
¼ teaspoon pepper
3 eggs
½ pound cooked crabmeat, flaked, or ½ pound finely chopped cooked shrimp

Preheat the oven to 450°.

Place the beer and butter in a saucepan. Bring mixture to a boil. When the butter is melted, add the flour, salt and pepper. Stir until well blended. Cook over low heat until the mixture begins to pull away from the sides of the pan.

Remove the saucepan from the heat and beat in the eggs, one at a time.

Drop the dough by heaping teaspoons 1 inch apart onto greased cookie sheets. Bake 10 minutes. Reduce heat to 350° and continue baking for 10 minutes longer or until golden brown. Cool slightly. Split the puffs and fill them with the crabmeat or shrimp.

serves 6 to 8

🌿 Cheese Straws

1 cup grated Parmesan cheese
1 cup flour
salt to taste
cayenne pepper to taste
1 tablespoon melted butter
1 egg yolk, beaten

Preheat the oven to 450°.

Combine the flour and cheese in a mixing bowl. Add the salt and cayenne. Add the beaten egg yolk and the melted butter. Mix gently to form a paste.

Roll the dough out onto a lightly floured surface to ⅛-inch thickness. With a pastry wheel or sharp knife, cut the dough into strips 4 inches long. Place the strips on heavily greased baking sheets and bake until light brown, about 5 to 7 minutes. Cool slightly and remove from sheets.

serves 6 to 8

🌿 Eggplant Caviar

1 large eggplant
1 large onion, chopped
1 green pepper, chopped
½ cup olive oil
1 large garlic clove, chopped
2 tomatoes, peeled and chopped
salt to taste
black pepper to taste
4 tablespoons white wine or dry vermouth

Preheat the oven to 400°.

Place the whole eggplant in a lightly oiled baking dish and bake until soft, about 1 hour.

In a skillet, sauté the onions and green pepper in the olive oil until soft but not brown. Add the garlic and cook 2 minutes longer. Do not brown.

When the eggplant is done, allow it to cool. Peel and chop the eggplant. Add it to the onion mixture. Add the chopped tomatoes. Season to taste with salt and pepper.

Add the wine and mix well. Cook until the mixture is thick, about 25 to 30 minutes.

Cool and chill for 8 hours or overnight. Serve with bread or crackers.

serves 8

🌿 Guacamole

2 large ripe avocados
1 large tomato, peeled, seeded and finely chopped
1 hard-cooked egg, finely chopped
½ cup finely chopped onions
2 canned green chilis, drained, seeded and finely chopped
1 tablespoon lemon juice
1 teaspoon salt

Cut the avocados in half and remove the pits. Peel off the skin (this can easily be done with your fingers). In a bowl coarsely chop the avocados and then mash them with a fork or the back of a spoon until smooth. Add the tomato, egg, onions, chilis, lemon juice and salt. Mix well.

Serve in a bowl with chips or tostadas for dipping.

🌿 Soups and Salads 🌿

I've always been partial to soups and salads as a quick and easy way to liven up an "on-the-spot" lunch or weekday dinner when you don't have the time to prepare something special. Try what I do: mix 'n match a soup recipe and a salad recipe and turn what would have been just another lunch into something surprising.

Try Corn and Shrimp Chowder with Crab and Fruit Salad or Beefy Okra Soup with a sandwich and Southern-Style Potato Salad. Or how about Cold Fruit Soup with a heaping bowl of Manor House Apple Salad for some hot summer afternoon when you'd rather do just about anything than stand there stirring a pot on a hot range. And if you find yourself with some time and you're in the mood to do something really creative, try the Shrimp and Bean Salad with Hambone Soup and a basketful of homemade bread.

You'll find that all these recipes are deliciously simple to cook and serve. Most of them, like the Crab Bisque, Cold Curry Soup, New Orleans Carrot Soup and Cream of Peanut Soup can even be made days or weeks ahead of time and frozen. And when you thaw and reheat them—either in the microwave or on top of the stove—they'll be just as satisfying and delicious as if you'd serve them piping hot from the soup pot.

🌿 Ham Hock and Cabbage Soup

1 to 1½ pounds smoked ham hocks
1 bay leaf
½ teaspoon black pepper
1½ cups whole stewed tomatoes
½ cabbage head, chopped
1 tablespoon vegetable oil
¼ pound beef, cubed
1 tablespoon flour
½ teaspoon salt
⅛ teaspoon Tabasco sauce

Put the ham hocks in a large pot and add the bay leaf and pepper. Add enough cold water to cover the ingredients. Bring the liquid to a boil, then reduce the heat, cover the pot and simmer for 1 hour.

Add the tomatoes and cabbage to the soup, stir well, and simmer for 1 hour longer. Remove the ham hocks, cut the meat from the bones and chop. Discard the bones; return the meat to the soup.

Heat the vegetable oil in a skillet. Add the cubed beef and sauté until lightly browned. Sprinkle the flour over the beef, stirring constantly with a wooden spoon. Spoon off 1 or 2 tablespoons of the soup broth and add to the skillet to loosen the gravy. Stir well. Add the beef and gravy to the soup. Stir in the salt and Tabasco sauce, cook for another 3 minutes, and serve.

serves 6

13

Hambone Soup

1 bone from a baked Virginia ham, with some
    meat still on it
1½ quarts cold water
½ cup chopped carrots
½ cup diced celery
½ cup chopped onions
½ cup whole kernel corn
½ cup lima beans, drained (thawed if frozen)
1 cup soaked black-eyed peas, with their liquid
1 cup whole stewed tomatoes
1 cup cooked elbow macaroni
⅛ teaspoon cayenne pepper
salt to taste

Break the bone into pieces about 2 inches
long. Put the bone pieces in a large soup
pot, add the water and simmer for 30
minutes.

Remove the bone pieces from the pot. Cut
off the meat and chop it into small pieces.
Return the meat (and the bones if desired)
to the pot. Add the carrots, celery and
onion and simmer the soup over a low heat
for 30 minutes.

Stir the soup, and add the corn, lima beans
and black-eyed peas. Simmer for 1½ hours,
or until the lima beans and black-eyed peas
are tender.

Add the macaroni, cayenne and salt. Simmer for 5 minutes longer, stirring frequently.

Serve hot with corn bread.

serves 8 to 10

Shrimp and Rice Soup

2 tablespoons olive oil
1 cup raw rice
1 cup chopped tomatoes
1 cup cooked shrimp, shelled and deveined
3 cups hot water
1 teaspoon salt
1 teaspoon Tabasco sauce

Heat the olive oil in a heavy skillet until
very hot. Add the rice and cook, stirring
constantly, until it turns a deep golden
brown. Add the tomatoes, shrimp, hot
water, salt and Tabasco sauce. Cover and
cook until the rice is tender and has
absorbed almost all the liquid, approximately 15 to 20 minutes.

serves 4

Corn and Shrimp Chowder

3 tablespoons butter
¼ cup chopped scallions
1 garlic clove, finely minced
¼ teaspoon black pepper
1½ cups light cream
½ cup water
2 potatoes, peeled and diced
¼ teaspoon salt
½ teaspoon dried parsley
2 cups milk
3 ounces cream cheese
1 cup whole kernel corn, drained
1½ pounds fresh shrimp, shelled, deveined and
    chopped

Melt the butter in a large heavy pot or
Dutch oven. Add the scallions, garlic and
pepper and sauté over low heat until the
scallions are tender but not browned.

Add the cream, water, potatoes, salt, parsley
and milk. Simmer for 15 to 20 minutes, or
until the potatoes are soft. Stir frequently so
the cream and milk do not form a skin. Do
not allow the mixture to come to a boil.

Soften the cream cheese with a fork, then
stir it into the soup. When the cream cheese
is fully blended, add the corn and shrimp.
Bring the soup slowly to a boil, then immediately reduce the heat and simmer for 5 to
10 minutes, or until the shrimp are white
and tender. Serve the chowder piping hot.

serves 8

❧ Corn Soup

6 ears fresh corn
2 cups water
1 quart milk
2 tablespoons butter
2 tablespoons flour
2 teaspoons Worcestershire sauce
1 teaspoon salt
½ teaspoon black pepper
1 egg yolk, beaten

Cut the corn kernels from the cob with a sharp knife. Scrape the cobs with the back of a knife to remove all the kernels. Set aside. Reserve the cobs.

Place the cobs in a large pot with the water. Bring the water to a boil and cook for 15 minutes. Remove the cobs and discard. Reserve the liquid.

Stir the corn kernels into the corn liquid. Cook over medium-low heat for 10 minutes. Stir in the milk.

In a small saucepan, melt the butter. Stir in the flour and combine until well blended. Add to the soup.

Add the Worcestershire sauce, salt and pepper to the soup. Mix well. Continue to cook for 5 more minutes. Slowly stir in the egg yolk. Remove from the heat and serve.

serves 4 to 6

❧ She-Crab Soup

6 tablespoons butter
1 tablespoon flour
2 cups milk
2 cups light cream
1 teaspoon freshly grated lemon rind
¼ teaspoon ground mace
1 pound white crabmeat and roe (if possible),
    picked and flaked
1 teaspoon salt
¼ teaspoon black pepper
3 tablespoons dry sherry
1 teaspoon finely chopped parsley

In the top of a double boiler over briskly boiling water, melt the butter. When melted, add the flour and blend well. Pour in the milk and light cream. Stir constantly. Add the grated lemon rind, mace and crabmeat and roe. Stir well and continue cooking for 20 minutes. Add the salt and pepper.

Remove the mixture from the heat and allow it to stand over the hot water for 15 minutes. Stir in the sherry and serve. Garnish each bowl with chopped parsley.

George Washington was served this soup on a visit to Charleston, South Carolina in 1791. The soup need not be made with female crabs and their roe; any crabmeat will do.

serves 6 to 8

🦐 Crab Bisque

½ pound crabmeat, picked and flaked
4 cups fish stock
1 cup unflavored breadcrumbs
1 onion, thinly sliced
2 parsley sprigs
1 bay leaf
¼ teaspoon dried thyme
2 tablespoons softened butter
1 cup heavy cream
salt to taste
black pepper to taste
⅛ teaspoon cayenne pepper
2 tablespoons chopped cooked shrimp
1 tablespoon sweet butter

In a large saucepan combine the fish stock, crabmeat, breadcrumbs, onion, parsley, bay leaf and thyme. Bring the mixture to a boil. Lower the heat and simmer gently for 20 minutes.

Strain the soup through a sieve and return the liquid to the saucepan. Discard the solids in the sieve. Add the softened butter and heat the soup just to the boiling point. Add the cream and season with salt, pepper, and cayenne. Heat the soup through, but do not let it boil.

Just before serving, stir in the shrimp and sweet butter. Serve hot.

serves 6

🥕 *Potage Crécy (New Orleans Carrot Soup)*

4 large carrots, peeled and finely chopped
2 large onions, finely chopped
1 medium-sized turnip, peeled and finely chopped
2 celery stalks, finely chopped
1 teaspoon cornstarch
2 whole cloves
1 tablespoon butter
¼ teaspoon dried thyme
salt to taste
black pepper to taste
6 cups water
8 cups boiling water
4 cups milk

Place the carrots, onions, turnip and celery in a large pot. Add the 6 cups of water. Bring the water to a boil and cook until the vegetables are tender, about 25 minutes.

When the vegetables are soft, drain and mash them. Press the mashed vegetables through a sieve with the back of a spoon. Discard any solids that remain in the sieve.

Return the mashed vegetables to the pot. Add the 8 cups boiling water, the cloves, butter and thyme. Cover and simmer gently for 15 minutes. Mix the cornstarch with 1 tablespoon of the milk and add it to the pot after the first 5 minutes.

In a saucepan heat the remaining milk to the boiling point. Add the milk to the vegetables and cook for 3 minutes longer. Season with salt and pepper to taste. Serve hot.

serves 4 to 6

Country Green Beans

Cold Curry Soup

Potage Crècy (*New Orleans Carrot Soup*)

🥄 Beefy Okra Soup

8 tablespoons butter
2 pounds lean chuck or other stewing beef, cut
 into 2-inch cubes
2 1-pound cans whole tomatoes, drained
1½ pounds fresh okra, thinly sliced
boiling water
2 cups cooked lima beans
2 cups diced cooked chicken
salt to taste
black pepper to taste

Melt the butter in a large, deep pot. Add the beef and brown well on all sides. Add the tomatoes and okra. Add enough boiling water to cover the mixture completely and simmer, covered, for 1 hour.

After the mixture has cooked for 1 hour, remove the cover. Add 4 more cups of boiling water. Continue cooking until the soup returns to the boil. Lower the heat and simmer, covered, until the okra and tomatoes are soft. Stir frequently and skim the soup while it cooks. Add the lima beans and chicken. Season to taste with salt and pepper. Serve in deep bowls.

serves 8

🥄 Mulligatawny Soup

1 3-pound chicken, cut into serving pieces
4 tablespoons butter
½ cup chopped carrots
½ cup chopped green pepper
2 green apples, cored and chopped
1 tablespoon flour
2 teaspoons curry powder
8 cups chicken broth
2 whole cloves
¼ cup chopped parsley
1 tablespoon sugar
¼ teaspoon black pepper
1½ teaspoons salt

Melt the butter in a large saucepan. Add the chicken pieces and sauté until well browned, about 5 to 8 minutes.

Add the carrots, green pepper and apples. Stir well. Continue cooking until the mixture is browned, about 8 minutes. Stir often.

Add the flour and curry powder. Mix well. Add the chicken broth, 1 cup at a time, stirring well after each addition. Add the cloves, sugar, pepper and salt. Continue cooking until the mixture comes to a boil. Lower the heat, cover the saucepan, and simmer until the chicken is very tender, about 30 to 35 minutes.

Remove the chicken pieces from the soup and let them cool.

Strain the soup through a sieve. Push the vegetables through the sieve with the back of a spoon. Place the soup back in the saucepan and heat. Discard any solids remaining in the sieve.

Remove the chicken from the bone, cut it into small pieces, and add them to the soup. Mix well and serve hot.

serves 6

🍲 Fried Okra Soup

2 cups fresh lima beans
2 cups fresh corn, cut from the cob
3 medium-sized potatoes, peeled and diced
¼ teaspoon black pepper
¼ teaspoon salt
6 medium-sized tomatoes, chopped
2 medium-sized onions, chopped
½ cup chopped celery
1 tablespoon sugar
¼ head cabbage, chopped
¼ pound bacon, diced
4 cups sliced fresh okra

Combine the lima beans, corn, potatoes, pepper, salt, tomatoes, onions, celery and sugar in a large pot. Add enough cold water to cover.

Cover the pot and simmer until the vegetables are almost tender, about 45 minutes. Add the cabbage and stir well. Remove the pot from the heat.

Fry the bacon in a skillet until it is browned. Add the bacon to the soup; reserve the drippings.

Brown the okra slices in the bacon drippings. Add the okra and the drippings to the soup.

If the soup is too thick, add more water. Simmer, covered, for 20 minutes longer. Serve hot.

serves 10

🍲 Williamsburg Cream of Peanut Soup

1 medium-sized onion, finely chopped
½ cup finely chopped celery
4 tablespoons butter
2 quarts chicken broth
1 cup smooth peanut butter
2 cups light cream
salt to taste
black pepper to taste
chopped peanuts for garnish

In a large skillet sauté the onion and celery in the butter until soft but not browned. Add the flour and stir well. Pour in 1 cup of the chicken broth and bring the mixture to a boil, stirring frequently.

Remove the mixture from the heat and place it, ½ cup at a time, in a blender or food processor. Blend until smooth. Return the blended mixture to the skillet and add the remaining chicken broth, the cream, and the peanut butter. Whisk while heating gently. Do not allow the mixture to boil. Season to taste with salt and pepper.

Serve hot or cold, garnished with chopped peanuts.

This dish is a specialty of the King's Arms Tavern at the Williamsburg restoration in Virginia. Diners there are served by waiters in authentic eighteenth-century garb.

serves 8

🍲 Potato Soup with Dumplings

Dumplings ingredients:
2 tablespoons butter
⅓ cup sifted flour
2 eggs, beaten
¼ teaspoon salt
nutmeg to taste
water

Soup ingredients:
4 tablespoons butter
1 white onion, finely chopped
4 cups cold water
2½ pounds new potatoes, peeled and diced
½ cup chopped celery
¼ teaspoon white pepper
2 fresh parsley sprigs, chopped
1 cup sour cream

To make the dumplings, cream the butter and the flour together in a mixing bowl until smooth. Add the eggs and stir in the salt and nutmeg, mixing until they are thoroughly blended into a batter. Add the water, a little at a time, if the batter is too thick to be spooned into the soup. Set the dumpling batter aside.

To make the soup, melt the butter in a large soup pot. Add the onion and sauté over low heat until the onion is tender but not browned. Add the cold water and bring it to a boil. Add the potatoes, celery, pepper and parsley and boil for 1 minute. Reduce the heat to low and simmer for 15 to 20 minutes, or until potatoes are soft when pricked with a fork.

Drop the dumpling batter by teaspoons into the soup. Cover the pot and simmer for about 10 minutes, or until the dumplings are bobbing on the surface of the soup.

Reduce heat to very low and slowly stir in the sour cream, stirring constantly until it is completely blended.

serves 10

❧ Cold Curry Soup

2 tablespoons butter
2 tablespoons curry powder
4 cups chicken broth
6 large egg yolks
½ cup light cream
½ cup heavy cream

In a large saucepan combine the butter and curry powder. Mix together and simmer over low heat for 5 minutes. Pour in the chicken broth and bring the mixture to a boil. Lower the heat and whisk in the egg yolks, light cream, and heavy cream. Stir constantly until the soup begins to thicken. Do not let the soup boil.

Chill and serve very cold.

serves 4

❧ Cold Fruit Soup

½ cup dried apricots
¼ cup dark raisins
¼ cup golden raisins
½ cup diced fresh peaches
2 cups water
1 cinnamon stick
4 cups apple cider
2 cups of mixed chopped fresh fruit, such as plums, strawberries, apricots, blueberries, nectarines and/or mangos

Place the dried apricots, dark and golden raisins and peaches in a deep saucepan. Add the water and the cinnamon stick. Simmer over medium heat for about 30 minutes or until the dried fruits are soft. Remove the cinnamon stick. Pour the fruit mixture into a blender or food processor and purée until smooth.

Pour the purée back into the saucepan. Return the cinnamon stick, add the apple cider, and simmer until hot. Add the mixed fresh fruits and cook for 5 or 10 minutes or until all the fruits are very soft. Remove the cinnamon stick.

Chill for 2 hours in refrigerator and serve cold.

serves 6

Stuffed Lettuce Head

1 large head iceberg lettuce
½ pound blue cheese
¼ pound sharp white Cheddar cheese, cut or
   crumbled into small pieces
3 ounces softened cream cheese
4 tablespoons light cream
3 hard-boiled egg yolks
1 tablespoon minced chives
1 tablespoon chopped scallion greens
1 red pimento, diced
10 green olives, sliced
¼ teaspoon Tabasco sauce

Remove any wilted or blemished leaves from the lettuce. Using a small knive, core the lettuce, making a hole about 3 inches wide and 3 inches deep (make sure your cutting doesn't break through the top of the lettuce head.)

Put the blue cheese, Cheddar cheese and cream cheese into a bowl and mash them together. Add the cream and mix well until a paste forms (use more cream if necessary). Mix in the egg yolks, chives, scallions, pimento, olives and Tabasco sauce. Mix well until all ingredients are thoroughly blended.

Spoon the cheese mixture into the hollowed part of the lettuce, filling the cavity and letting the dressing drip down over the outside leaves. Sprinkle with paprika and bacon bits, chill, and serve.

serves 6

Wilted Lettuce

6 slices bacon, diced
⅓ cup cider vinegar
2 heads lettuce, torn into medium-small pieces
¼ cup chopped scallions
¼ teaspoon salt
¼ teaspoon black pepper
2 hard-cooked eggs, chopped

Sauté the bacon pieces in a large skillet. When the bacon is crisp, add the vinegar to the skillet. Cook over very low heat until heated through.

Remove the skillet from the heat and add the lettuce, scallions, salt and pepper. Toss for 1 to 2 minutes, or until the lettuce is wilted. Add the chopped eggs and toss again. Place in a bowl and serve immediately.

serves 4

Dandelion Salad

1 pound young dandelion greens or arugala
5 slices bacon, diced
2 eggs
½ cup light cream
2 tablespoons butter
4 tablespoons vinegar
1 tablespoon sugar
1 teaspoon salt
½ teaspoon paprika
½ teaspoon black pepper

Wash and trim the dandelions. Place the leaves in a salad bowl and let stand in a warm place.

Fry the bacon in a small skillet. Pour the bacon fat and pieces over the dandelions.

Place the butter and light cream in a saucepan. Cook over low heat until the butter melts.

In a separate bowl, beat the eggs. Add the pepper, salt, paprika, vinegar and sugar. Add this mixture to the cream and butter mixture. Stir until the mixture is very hot and thickens to the consistency of a custard. Pour over the dandelions and toss well.

serves 4

❧ Crab and Fruit Salad

1 pound cooked crabmeat, picked and flaked
1 navel orange, peeled, sectioned and chopped
½ cup drained mandarin orange slices
½ cup chopped celery
½ cup seedless white grapes, cut in half
¼ teaspoon dried dill
salt to taste
black pepper to taste
½ cup mayonnaise
slivered almonds

Mix the crabmeat, orange pieces, mandarin orange sections, celery, grapes, and dill in a large salad bowl. Mix in the mayonnaise, a little at a time, until it lightly coats all the ingredients in the bowl. Season with salt and pepper. Sprinkle the almond slivers on top and serve chilled.

serves 4

❧ Manor House Apple Salad

2 cups diced firm, sweet apples
3 tablespoons fresh lemon juice
1 cup diced celery
½ cup chopped walnuts
1 cup chopped, pitted dates
salt to taste
black pepper to taste
¾ cup mayonnaise
1 teaspoon honey, thinned with ½ teaspoon warm water

In a large salad bowl, pour the lemon juice over the apples and mix thoroughly with a wooden spoon. Let the apples marinate in the juice for 15 minutes. Add the celery, walnuts, dates, salt, pepper and honey. Mix gently and serve well chilled on lettuce leaves.

serves 6

❧ Herbed Bean Salad

4 cups water
1 cup dried navy or pea beans
1 teaspoon salt
1 tablespoon taragon vinegar
2 teaspoons Dijon-style mustard
½ teaspoon Tabasco sauce
½ teaspoon black pepper
⅓ cup olive oil
2 tablespoons finely chopped fresh basil or 1 teaspoon dried crumbled basil
2 tablespoons finely chopped chives
2 finely chopped mint sprigs or ½ teaspoon dried crumbled mint
2 garlic cloves, finely chopped
1 large tomato, peeled, seeded, and coarsely chopped

In a large saucepan bring the water to a rapid boil. Add the navy beans and boil, uncovered, for 3 minutes. Remove the saucepan from the heat and let the beans cool in their liquid for 1 hour. Add the salt to liquid and bring the beans back to a boil. Lower the heat and simmer the beans, partially covered, for 1 hour or until they are tender. Remove from heat, drain, and cool.

In a mixing bowl, combine the vinegar, mustard, Tabasco, salt and pepper. Add the olive oil in a steady stream and whisk the mixture until smooth.

Ina large bowl combine the basil, chives, parsley, mint and garlic. Mix well. Add the beans and tomatoes. Stir gently but thoroughly.

Pour the tomato and bean mixture into the dressing. Toss the mixture until the pieces are well coated. Cover the bowl and chill for 5 hours. Remove from refrigerator 1 hour before serving.

serves 6

Spicy Chickpea Salad

4 cups cooked chickpeas (garbanzos)
1 small onion, finely chopped
1 tablespoon finely chopped parsley
2 medium-sized carrots, cooked and diced
¼ cup olive oil
2 tablespoons cider vinegar
1 teaspoon salt
½ teaspoon black pepper
1½ teaspoons hot red pepper flakes
⅛ teaspoon cayenne pepper
lettuce leaves

Drain the chickpeas well. Drain well.

In a large bowl, mix together the chickpeas, onion, parsley, carrots, oil, vinegar and red pepper flakes. Add the salt, pepper and cayenne.

Chill in refrigerator for 1 to 2 hours. When ready to serve, line a large serving bowl with lettuce and spoon in the salad.

serves 4

Southern-Style Potato Salad

6 medium potatoes
½ cup sweet pickles, finely chopped
1 medium-sized onion, finely chopped
½ cup cider vinegar
½ cup finely chopped celery
½ teaspoon Dijon-style mustard
1 teaspoon salt
¼ teaspoon black pepper
1½ cups mayonnaise

Place the potatoes in a pot with enough boiling salted water to cover. Cook, uncovered, until the potatoes are tender, about 40 minutes. Drain potatoes and allow to cool. When cool enough to handle, peel and dice into small cubes.

Place the diced potatoes in a large bowl. Add the cider vinegar and mix gently.

In a separate bowl combine the celery, onion, pickles, salt, pepper, mustard, and mayonnaise. Add the potato mixture and combine gently. Season to taste and let stand, covered, for 2 hours before serving to let flavors combine.

serves 6

Vegetable Salad

1 cucumber, peeled and sliced
½ cup cooked lima beans
½ cup cooked diced carrots
6 pimiento-stuffed olives, sliced
¾ cup mayonnaise
1 teaspoon chili sauce
¼ teaspoon sugar
½ teaspoon prepared horseradish
½ teaspoon salt
5 large lettuce leaves
2 tablespoons olive oil
1 tomato, finely chopped
4 scallions, chopped

In a large bowl combine the cucumber, lima beans, carrots, olives, mayonnaise, chili sauce, sugar, horseradish and salt. Mix well.

Place the lettuce leaves in a bowl. Add the olive oil and toss.

Line a serving bowl with the lettuce leaves. Add the vegetable mixture to the bowl. Top with the chopped scallions and chopped tomato. Serve immediately.

serves 4

❦ Cabbage Salad

1 large head cabbage, shredded
1 green pepper, coarsely chopped
¼ cup mayonnaise
¼ cup sour cream
3 tablespoons white wine vinegar
3 tablespoons sugar
½ teaspoon chili powder
½ teaspoon salt
¼ teaspoon black pepper
⅛ teaspoon cayenne pepper

Place the shredded cabbage in a large bowl and add the green pepper. Mix well and chill.

In a mixing bowl combine the mayonnaise, sour cream, vinegar, sugar, chili powder, salt, pepper and cayenne pepper. Blend well and chill for 2 hours.

Pour the dressing over the cabbage mixture and toss very well. Serve chilled.

serves 6

❦ Green Bean Salad

2 pounds whole fresh green beans
½ pound salt pork, sliced
6 tablespoons wine vinegar
¾ cup olive oil
2 medium-sized onions, finely chopped
salt to taste
black pepper to taste

Trim the green beans and blanch them in a large pot of boiling water for 3 to 5 minutes. Drain and rinse with cold water.

In a small skillet cook the salt pork until it is well browned and crisp. Remove the salt pork from the skillet and crumble.

In a large bowl combine the vinegar, olive oil, onions, salt and pepper. Add the green beans and toss well. Chill for 2 to 3 hours.

Drain the beans and place them in a serving bowl. Add the crumbled salt pork. Toss well and serve.

serves 6

❦ Florida Seafood Salad

16 large cooked shrimp, peeled and deveined
½ cup coarsely chopped cooked lobster
½ cup cooked crabmeat, flaked
½ cup cooked scallops (cut in half if they are large)
1 grapefruit, peeled and sectioned
½ cup black or green olives
½ cup olive oil
1½ teaspoons white wine vinegar
½ teaspoon Dijon-style mustard
¼ teaspoon salt
⅛ teaspoon black pepper

Place the shrimp, lobster, crabmeat, and scallops in a bowl and chill.

Into a large bowl lined with lettuce or spinach leaves place the shrimp, lobster, crabmeat, and scallops. Add the grapefruit sections and olives.

In a small bowl combine the vinegar, mustard, salt, and pepper. Whisk in the oil until well blended.

Pour dressing over salad and toss lightly. Serve immediately.

serves 4

🦋 Papaya Seafood Salad

2 ripe papayas, chilled
2 cups chopped cooked shrimp or flaked
    crabmeat
1 cup chopped celery
½ teaspoon curry powder
½ cup mayonnaise
juice of 1 lime
1 lime, quartered

Cut the papayas in half and scoop out the seeds.

In a bowl combine the shrimp, celery, curry powder, and mayonnaise. Fill each papaya half with the mixture. Sprinkle with the lime juice. Serve each papaya with a lime wedge.

Papayas are low in calories but high in vitamins. They grow in the Caribbean and are extremely popular throughout the South and Southwest. Most well-stocked supermarkets carry papayas.

serves 4

🦋 Shrimp and Bean Salad

1 cup cooked white beans
1 cup cooked kidney beans
¾ pound cooked shrimp, peeled and deveined
1 cup finely chopped green pepper
1 tablespoon chopped onions
1 tablespoon chopped pimento
½ teaspoon salt
¼ teaspoon black pepper
⅛ teaspoon cayenne pepper
¼ cup white wine vinegar
½ cup olive oil

If using canned beans, place them in a colander and rinse under cold running water. Drain well.

In a large bowl combine the beans, shrimp, green pepper, onions, and pimento. Sprinkle salt, pepper, and cayenne over the salad.

In a mixing bowl combine the vinegar and olive oil. Whisk until well blended.

Pour only enough oil and vinegar over the salad to moisten it well. Toss. Chill for 1 hour and serve.

serves 4

Meat and Poultry

If you and your family are used to meat dinners with plain old steak, pot roast, chops or fried chicken, you've got to come South for some real home cookin'. But until you can make the trip, here are some meat and poultry recipes that'll make you swear you can smell the magnolias.

They say that sitting down to a dinner in the South is like going to heaven…with second helpings. They're not far wrong. The recipes in these pages will prove my statement. Say you like your chicken sweet and succulent…well, Fruit 'n' Honey Chicken or Key West Lime Chicken will taste like answers to prayers. Or maybe you'd like to tempt the family, those special friends, and of course, yourself, with such mouth-watering feasts as Sherried Smithfield Ham, Creole Roast Pork, Chicken-Fried Steak with Spicy Gravy, truly classic Southern Fried Chicken, or a serving dish piled to the sky with authentic Jambalaya!

Chicken-Fried Steak with Spicy Gravy

6 8-ounce steaks, about ½ inch thick
1½ teaspoons salt
½ teaspoon black pepper
flour
milk
vegetable shortening
Spicy Gravy:
pan drippings from steaks
3 cups milk
6 tablespoons butter
¼ teaspoon cayenne pepper
2 dashes Tabasco sauce
1½ teaspoons salt
½ cup flour

Score the steaks crosswise on both sides with a sharp knife. Pound the steaks with a mallet until they are about ¼ inch thick.

Dust the steaks with the salt and pepper, then dredge each steak in the flour. Dip the coated steaks in the milk, and then dredge again in the flour.

Melt the shortening in a skillet over medium heat. Add the steaks and fry for about 3 minutes (less for rare meat) on each side, pressing the steaks down on the skillet with a spatula from time to time. Remove the steaks when done and keep them warm.

To make the spicy gravy, heat the milk in a large saucepan over very low heat. Don't let the milk boil or form a skin.

Reduce the heat under the skillet with the steak drippings. Add the butter, cayenne pepper, Tabasco sauce and salt. Stir for 1 minute. Slowly blend in the flour until the mixture becomes a roux.

Slowly pour the roux into the heated milk, stirring constantly so it blends evenly. Simmer the gravy (do not let it boil) until it thickens to your taste. Serve in a gravy boat with the steaks.

serves 6

❧ Creoles Grillades

1 to 1½ pounds beef round, approximately
    ½-inch thick
salt to taste
black pepper to taste
⅛ teaspoon cayenne pepper
2 tablespoons lard or olive oil
1 small onion, thinly sliced
2 garlic cloves, finely chopped
1 large tomato, chopped

Trim the fat from the meat. Cut it into 3- or 4-inch squares. Place the meat squares between two sheets of waxed paper. Using a meat mallet, pound the squares until they are about ¼-inch thick. Rub the meat on both sides with salt, pepper and cayenne.

In a large, heavy skillet heat the lard or oil. Add the onion and garlic and sauté, stirring constantly, until brown, about 5 to 7 minutes. Stir in the tomato and cook for 2 minutes.

Add the meat and stir well to coat on all sides. Cover the skillet and cook for 10 minutes, or until the beef is tender and well browned. Serve hot.

Traditionally served in New Orleans as a breakfast dish with grits, this is also a good main course when served with beans or rice.

serves 4 to 6

❧ Creole-Style Breaded Oxtails

2 oxtails
3 teaspoons chopped parsley
½ teaspoon dried thyme
1 bay leaf
salt to taste
black pepper to taste
cayenne pepper to taste
1 egg
1 cup breadcrumbs
oil for frying

Wash the oxtails and cut them at the joints. Cut each piece into two pieces about 4 inches long.

Fill a saucepan with water and bring it to a boil. Add the parsley, thyme, bay leaf, salt, pepper and cayenne. Add the oxtails, cover and boil until they are tender, about 2½ to 3 hours. Remove the saucepan from the heat and let the oxtails cool in the cooking liquid.

In a mixing bowl, beat the egg. Dip the pieces of oxtail into the egg and then roll them in the breadcrumbs.

Place a layer of oil 1 inch deep into a deep skillet. Heat until the oil is very hot. Add the breaded oxtail pieces and fry until they are golden brown, about 5 to 7 minutes.

Remove the oxtails and drain them on paper towels. Serve with tartar sauce if desired.

Roast Leg of Lamb with Sweet Potatoes

¼ cup tarragon vinegar
2 tablespoons water
1½ cups water
salt to taste
black pepper to taste
2 garlic cloves, finely chopped
¼ teaspoon dried dill
1 5½- to 6-pound leg of lamb, boned
½ cup apple cider
8 medium-sized sweet potatoes
2 tablespoons butter
1 teaspoon grated orange peel
2 teaspoons lemon juice
1 cup chopped apples
½ cup chopped pecans
3 tablespoons brown sugar

In a mixing bowl, combine the vinegar, 2 tablespoons water, salt, pepper, garlic and dill. Mix thoroughly.

Place the leg of lamb in a shallow dish. Pour the marinade over the lamb. Marinate in the refrigerator for 8 hours or overnight, turning occasionally.

Preheat the oven to 350°.

Remove the lamb from the marinade and place it in a baking dish. Bake for 2½ hours. Pour off the drippings in the pan and reserve.

Combine the 1½ cups water and the apple cider in a bowl. Pour the mixture over the lamb and bake 30 minutes longer.

Bake the sweet potatoes in the oven with the lamb for 1 hour or until they are tender. When the sweet potatoes are cool enough to handle, cut them lengthwise and scoop out the pulp. Reserve the shells.

In a bowl, mash the sweet potatoes with the butter and orange peel. Add the lemon juice and apples to the mixture. Stir in the pecans and mix well. Spoon the mixture back into the sweet potato shells. Sprinkle with brown sugar. If there is any sweet potato mixture left, stuff the lamb cavity with it.

Place the sweet potato halves into a shallow baking dish and bake for 15 to 20 minutes.

To make a gravy, skim the fat from the reserved pan drippings.

Serve the lamb on a platter surrounded by the stuffed sweet potato shells.

serves 8 to 10

Creole-Style Stewed Kidneys

3 to 5 beef or pork kidneys
1½ tablespoons butter
1 cup beef broth
salt to taste
black pepper to taste
1 teaspoon chopped parsley
½ teaspoon dried thyme
1 bay leaf
1 cup water
½ cup white wine

Remove the white membrane from the kidneys and wash the kidneys well. Pat them dry and slice them very thinly.

Melt the butter in a saucepan. When it is very hot, add the kidneys, salt, pepper, parsley, thyme and bay leaf. Stir constantly and quickly to prevent burning. Cook briefly, no more than 3 minutes.

Add the wine, water and beef broth. Heat the mixture just to the boiling point. The entire cooking time for this dish should not exceed 5 minutes. Serve immediately.

serves 4

🦋 Liver and Bacon

1 pound fresh calf's liver
½ pound slab bacon
1 tablespoon flour
½ teaspoon salt
black pepper to taste
parsley for garnish

Slice the liver into pieces about 3 inches long and ¼-inch thick. Slice the bacon very thinly, making the same number of slices as there are pieces of liver.

Brown the bacon in a skillet. Remove and set aside in a warm place.

Season the flour with the salt and pepper. Dust the liver pieces with the flour. Sauté the liver in the bacon fat for about 2½ to 3 minutes per side.

Remove the liver from the pan and arrange it on a serving platter in alternate slices with the bacon. Garnish with parsley and serve.

serves 4

🦋 Dried Beef and Gravy

½ pound dried beef
2 tablespoons butter
2 tablespoons bacon fat
5 tablespoons flour
3 cups milk
4 potatoes
1 cup potato water
salt to taste
black pepper to taste

Boil the potatoes in enough water to cover in a saucepan until they are tender, about 20 to 25 minutes. Drain well, reserving 1 cup of the cooking water. Peel and quarter the potatoes and set them aside.

Break the dried beef into small pieces and place them in a medium-sized skillet. Add enough water to cover. Add the butter and bacon fat. Bring the liquid to a boil and cook until the water has boiled away and the beef has frizzled brown in the fat.

Lower the heat and stir in the flour, milk, potato water, salt and pepper. Continue cooking until the mixture is thick and smooth.

Mash the boiled potatoes with butter and a little milk. Serve the beef over the potatoes.

serves 4 to 6

🦋 Caldillo

1 pound stewing beef, cubed
¾ cup diced onion
2 tablespoons bacon fat or olive oil
1½ cups diced tomatoes
¾ cup sliced green chili peppers
¼ cup beef broth
¼ cup water
1 teaspoon salt
1 teaspoon black pepper
2 garlic cloves, chopped
1 teaspoon ground cumin
1 pound potatoes, peeled and cubed

Heat the bacon fat or olive oil in a heavy skillet. Add the beef and onions. Sauté until the onions are soft but not brown, about 5 to 8 minutes. Add the tomatoes, chilis, beef broth, water, salt, pepper, garlic and cumin. Cook, covered, over low heat until the meat is tender, about 2 hours. Add the potatoes after the mixture has cooked for 1½ hours.

serves 4 to 6

❧ Picadillo

2 tablespoons olive oil
1 large onion, thinly sliced
3 garlic cloves, finely chopped
½ pound lean ground beef
½ pound ground pork
salt to taste
black pepper to taste
¼ teaspoon ground cumin
1 bay leaf
½ cup red wine
2 large tomatoes, peeled and chopped
¼ cup dark raisins
1 sweet red pepper, cut into strips

In a large deep skillet heat the olive oil. Add the onion and garlic. Cook, stirring constantly, until they are soft and golden, about 5 to 7 minutes. Add the beef, pork, salt, pepper and cumin. Mix well. Cook over low heat, stirring constantly, until the meat is well browned.

Add the bay leaf, wine, tomatoes and raisins. Mix well and cover the skillet. Simmer the mixture over low heat for 15 minutes, stirring frequently. If the mixture is too wet, remove the cover and continue cooking. Stir in the red pepper strips and cook 2 minutes longer.

Serve over rice or use the mixture to fill taco shells.

serves 4

❧ Orange Grove Pork Chops

4 8-ounce center-cut pork chops
salt to taste
black pepper to taste
flour for dredging
3 tablespoons butter
1 large orange, peeled and cut into thin slices
½ cup orange juice
watercress (optional)

Rub the pork chops with the salt and pepper. Dredge them in the flour. Shake off any excess flour.

Heat the butter in a large skillet. Add the chops and quickly brown them over high heat, about 3 to 5 minutes per side. Remove the chops and transfer them to a large shallow baking dish. The dish should be large enough to hold all the chops in one layer.

Preheat the oven to 350°.

Top each pork chop with 1 or 2 orange slices. Cover the dish tightly with aluminum foil. Bake for 1 hour or until the chops are tender. Serve the chops on a bed of watercress.

serves 4

❧ Double-Deck Pork Tostadas

1 pound ground pork
1 medium-sized onion, chopped
1½ teaspoons chili powder
1 teaspoon salt
¼ teaspoon ground cumin
1 garlic clove, finely chopped
2 cups cooked kidney beans, mashed
¼ cup bean cooking liquid
½ cup water
8 6-inch corn tortillas
1 cup shredded lettuce
½ cup shredded mild cheese
1 tomato, chopped

Brown the pork and onion together in a large skillet. Pour off the fat. Add the chili powder, salt, cumin and garlic.

Add the mashed beans to the pork. Stir in the bean liquid and water. Cook slowly for 15 minutes, stirring occasionally.

Heat the tortillas according to the package directions.

Spread about ⅓ cup of the pork mixture on each of 4 tortillas; place ¼ cup of lettuce over each. Top each with a second tortilla. Spread each with an equal portion of the remaining pork mixture. Top with the shredded cheese and chopped tomato.

Prepared tortillas are easily found in most supermarkets.

serves 4

❧ Country Style Ham

1 10-ounce fresh country ham, soaked and scrubbed
2 cups dark molasses
4 ounces brandy
4 cups strong tea
1 tablespoon dry mustard
½ cup chili or hot sauce
ground cloves
ground ginger

Put the ham in a very large roasting pan on top of the stove. Spread the molasses over the ham, covering it completely. Pour the brandy over the ham, then pour enough tea over it so that about half the ham is beneath the surface of the liquid.

Put the pan over two stove burners, cover and simmer over medium heat for 1½ hours. Turn the ham over and simmer for another 1½ hours.

Remove the roasting pan from the heat. Skin the ham and let it cool in the cooking liquid in the pan.

Mix the mustard and chili or hot sauce together in a small bowl. Place the ham on a rack set in a roasting pan. Dust the ham with the ground cloves and ginger, then brush the mustard and chili sauce mixture over the ham.

Preheat the oven to 400°. Bake the ham for 30 minutes. Reduce the oven temperature to 350° and bake for another 45 minutes, or until the ham bone is yielding when moved.

Serve hot or cold.

serves 20

🌿 Sherried Smithfield Ham

1 14-pound Smithfield ham
½ pound brown sugar
1 cup sherry

Wash the ham well and place it in a large pan, skin-side down. Cover the ham completely with cold water. Soak for 2 days, changing the water after the first day.

Drain the ham and place it in a large, top-of-the-stove roasting pan. Cover the ham completely with cold water. Simmer the ham for 25 minutes per pound, about 4 hours.

When the ham is done, let it cool in the cooking liquid. Remove the skin.

Preheat the oven to 350°.

Dissolve the brown sugar in the sherry in a small bowl.

Place the ham in a large baking dish and bake for 20 to 30 minutes, or until the ham is heated through. When the ham is hot, poke holes with a skewer into the side where the skin was removed. Pour some of the sherry mixture into the holes. Return the ham to the oven and continue to pour the sherry into the holes every few minutes until the mixture is used up.

Remove the ham from the oven and allow to cool slightly. Slice the ham as thinly as possible and serve.

Smithfield hams have been made in Tidewater Virginia for more than 350 years. These superb hams are made from peanut-fed pigs. The hams are cured in salt for 35 days, then set aside for another 21 days. They are then air-cured for 6 months or longer.

serves 16 to 20

🌿 Southern-Style Baked Ham

1 10-pound fresh uncooked ham
1 tablespoon whole cloves
1 stick cinnamon
1 cup sugar
1¼ cups white vinegar
2 garlic cloves
1 onion
1 cup dark brown sugar
2 teaspoons dry mustard
¾ cup water

Wash the ham and place it in a large saucepan with enough cold water to cover. Add the cloves, cinnamon stick, sugar, 1 cup vinegar, garlic and onion. Bring the mixture to a boil, reduce the heat, and simmer for 2½ hours.

Remove the ham from the saucepan and let it cool at room temperature for 3 hours.

Preheat the oven to 350°.

Remove the skin from the ham. Dry the ham gently but thoroughly.

In a small bowl combine the brown sugar and dry mustard. Rub the mixture into the ham. Place the ham in a large baking dish and add the remaining vinegar and the water to the dish. Bake the ham for 1 hour. After the ham has cooked for 30 minutes, baste it every 7 to 10 minutes with the liquid in the baking dish.

serves 10 to 12

❧ Creole Roast Pork

1 6-pound loin of pork roast
1 teaspoon salt
½ teaspoon pepper
1 teaspoon dried sage
8 large tart apples, cored
4 cooked sweet potatoes, peeled and quartered
2 tablespoons brown sugar
¼ teaspoon grated nutmeg
¼ cup melted butter
¼ cup pure maple sugar

Preheat the oven to 300°.

Sprinkle the meat with the salt, pepper and sage. Rub the seasonings into the meat. Place the roast, fat-side up, on a rack in a baking pan. Roast for 3 hours.

With a sharp knife, remove enough pulp from the apples to make the core opening 1½ to 2 inches wide. Chop the removed pulp and reserve.

In a large bowl, mash the sweet potatoes. Add the apple pulp, brown sugar, nutmeg and pepper.

In a small saucepan, heat the butter and maple sugar. Cook for 2 minutes. Spoon 1 teaspoon of the mixture into each of the apples. Reserve the leftover syrup.

Fill the apple openings with the sweet potato mixture until the apples are very full.

Remove the roast from the oven. Drain the fat from the pan and place the apples around the roast. Roast for 1½ hours longer. Baste the apples frequently with the reserved syrup. When the roast is done, place it on a serving platter and surround it with the apples.

serves 6 to 8

❧ Roast Pork with Turnips

1 3½-pound smoked pork shoulder
1½ pounds turnips, peeled and quartered
2 tablespoons cider vinegar
salt to taste
black pepper to taste

Preheat the oven to 325°.

Tie the pork tightly with string and place in a lightly oiled roasting pan. Roast for 1 hour.

After the pork has roasted for 50 minutes, begin to cook the turnips. Steam the turnips in a steamer or a little bit of water. Bring the water to a boil, then lower the heat and simmer, covered, for 8 to 10 minutes.

When the pork has roasted for 1 hour, add the turnips to the roasting pan and mix them with the pork drippings. Return the roast to the oven for 30 minutes.

Remove the pork to a cutting board. Pour the vinegar over the turnips in the roasting pan and mix well. Slice the pork and serve surrounded with turnips.

serves 4 to 6

Shrimp in Beer

Avocado Appetizer

Southern-Style Potato Salad

Orange Grove Pork Chops

Corn and Okra Mix

Guacamole with Tortillas

🌿 Spiced Fresh Ham

1 10-pound fresh ham
1 tablespoon ground cinnamon
1 tablespoon ground nutmeg
1 tablespoon ground ginger
1½ teaspoons salt
½ teaspoon freshly ground black pepper
6 cups white flour
1 cup warm water
2 quarts apple cider
2 eggs, beaten
3 cups unflavored bread crumbs
½ cup currant jelly

Wash the ham in warm water and dry thoroughly. In a small bowl, mix the cinnamon, nutmeg, ginger, salt and pepper together. Rub the mixture vigorously into the ham.

Put the flour into a mixing bowl. Add just enough water to form a stiff dough. Mix well. Put the dough on a lightly floured surface and roll it out to form a ¼-inch thick crust. Wrap the ham in the dough. Pinch all the edges sealed.

Preheat the oven to 325°. Place the wrapped ham, fat-side up, in a roasting pan. Pour the apple cider into the pan and bake, uncovered, for 2¼ hours, basting often.

Remove the ham from the oven. Peel off and discard the dough wrapping. Cut away and discard the ham rind.

Pour the juices from the roasting pan into a saucepan. Pour ¼ cup of the juices over the ham to moisten it, then sprinkle the ham with the bread crumbs until it is completely covered. Return the ham to the oven and bake at 325° for 20 minutes longer.

While the ham is baking again, bring the juices in the saucepan to a boil. Add the currant jelly and stir with a whisk until the gravy is smooth and well blended. Strain the gravy into a sauceboat and serve with the ham.

serves 12

🌿 Ham and Apple Pie

2 pounds cooked ham, diced
5 tart apples, cored and sliced
¼ cup light brown sugar
⅛ teaspoon salt
½ teaspoon cinnamon
2 tablespoons butter
2 tablespoons lemon juice
¼ cup apple cider
1 unbaked 9-inch pastry shell

Preheat the oven to 375°.

Combine the sugar, salt, and cinnamon in a small bowl; mix well.

Butter a deep baking dish. Place alternate layers of ham and apples in the dish, sprinkling each layer with the sugar mixture and dotting each with butter. Be sure to end with a layer of apples.

Combine the lemon juice and apple cider in a small bowl. Pour over the top layer of apples. Cover the baking dish and bake in oven for 20 minutes.

At the end of 20 minutes, remove the dish from the oven and uncover it. Fit the pastry over the top of the dish. Crimp around the edge and flute. Cut a few slits in the center. Return the dish to the oven for 25 minutes longer, or until the pastry is golden.

serves 4

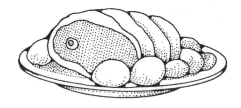

❧ Jambalaya

3 3-pound chickens, cut into serving pieces
flour for dredging
4 tablespoons lard or bacon fat
3 cups chopped onions
2 cups chopped sweet red pepper
1 scallion, thinly sliced
2 garlic cloves, chopped
½ pound lean baked ham, cut into ½-inch
    squares
1½ pound lean pork, trimmed of fat and cut
    into ½-inch cubes
6 hot sausages, thinly sliced
½ pound cooked shrimp, peeled and deveined
3 teaspoons salt
1 teaspoon black pepper
½ teaspoon Tabasco sauce
4 bay leaves
1½ cups raw long-grain rice
2 cups hot chicken broth
1 cup hot water

Wash the chicken pieces and remove all the
fat and skin. If the breasts are very large, cut
them in half. Dredge the chicken in the
flour and shake off any excess.

In a large deep casserole, heat the lard or
bacon fat. Add the chicken and quickly
brown the pieces on all sides over high heat.
Turn frequently, using tongs.

Remove the browned chicken pieces to a
warm place. To the casserole add the
onions, red pepper, scallions, garlic, ham
and pork. Reduce the heat to medium and
cook, stirring constantly, for 10 to 15 minutes, or until both the vegetables and ham
are browned. Add the sausage slices to the
casserole. Stir in the salt, pepper and bay
leaves. Cook, stirring constantly, for 4 minutes.

Return the chicken pieces to the pot. Stir in
the shrimp, raw rice, hot chicken broth and
hot water. Mix well. Raise the heat and
bring the mixture to a boil. Immediately
reduce the heat to very low. Cover the pot
and cook for 20 minutes, stirring occasionally. Uncover the casserole, raise the heat to
medium, and cook, stirring often, for 10
minutes longer, or until the rice is fluffy and
dry. Serve immediately.

This dish is best when made for a crowd.
An amalgam of French and Spanish cook-
ing traditions, jambalaya is a distinctively
Cajun dish.

serves 6 to 8

❧ Bayou Chicken Pie

4 cups cold cooked chicken, cut to bite-sized
    pieces
1 cup cooked sliced carrots
1 large yam, cooked, peeled and sliced
2 cups cooked onion slices
2 tablespoons chopped parsley
1 teaspoon chopped fresh dill or ¼ teaspoon
    dried dill
1½ cups chicken broth
1 cup light cream
4 tablespoons flour
salt to taste
black pepper to taste
Crust ingredients:
2 cups all-purpose flour
1 teaspoon baking powder
½ teaspoon salt
½ cup butter, softened
1 cup mashed yams
1 egg, beaten

Grease a large casserole or baking dish (over
2 quarts) with butter. Spread a layer of half
the chicken pieces on the bottom. On top of
the chicken, spread the parsley in a layer,
then the carrots, onion and yams. Top with
a final layer of the remaining chicken.

Pour enough light cream into medium-sized saucepan to cover the bottom. Over low heat, gradually blend in the flour until smooth. Slowly add the remaining cream and chicken stock, stirring constantly. Simmer the sauce, stirring constantly, over low heat for 2 to 3 minutes or until the sauce has thickened.

Dust the chicken and vegetables with salt and pepper to taste, and pour the sauce over them.

To make the crust, mix the flour, baking powder and salt together in a mixing bowl. Cut in the softened butter with a pastry blender or two knives until the mixture is grainy and resembles a coarse meal. Blend in the mashed yams and mix well. Add the egg and mix again.

Preheat the oven to 350°.

Roll the dough out on a lightly floured surface to a thickness of about ¼ inch.

Fit the crust over the casserole dish. Pinch the edges all around and pierce the center of the crust two or three times with a fork.

Bake the pie for 45 minutes to 1 hour, or until the crust is golden and flaky and the filling is bubbling.

serves 8

🐾 French Chicken

3 pounds chicken breasts, split
salt to taste
black pepper to taste
3 tablespoons butter
¼ pound Roquefort cheese
2 teaspoons minced garlic
1 teaspoon dried dill
4 ounces dry white wine
4 ounces sour cream

Dust the chicken breasts with salt and pepper. Melt the butter in a skillet over medium heat. Add the chicken breasts and sauté until both sides are light brown and the meat is opaque.

Remove the breasts from the skillet and put them in a large baking dish. Reserve the drippings.

Preheat the oven to 350°.

Heat the drippings in the skillet and add the cheese, garlic and dill. Stir with a wooden spoon until the cheese begins to soften and the ingredients are blended. Add the white wine and stir. Slowly add the sour cream while stirring. Heat the sauce until thoroughly blended, but do not let it boil.

Pour the sauce over the chicken breasts. Bake for 1 hour.

serves 6

❦ Fruit 'n' Honey Chicken

½ cup apple cider
½ cup fresh orange juice
¼ cup pineapple juice
¼ cup lemon juice
½ medium-sized white onion, diced
1 3-pound frying chicken, cut into serving pieces
salt to taste
black pepper to taste
peanut or safflower oil
honey
1 red apple, cored and sliced
½ cup white raisins
½ cup dried peaches or apricots
4 pitted prunes, sliced
¼ cup seedless red grapes

Mix the apple juice, orange juice, pineapple juice and onion in a mixing bowl. Add the chicken pieces and marinate for 1½ hours.

Remove the chicken from the marinade. Reserve the marinade. Dust the chicken parts with the salt and black pepper. Heat a thin layer of oil in a skillet. Add the chicken pieces and sauté until the parts are a light golden brown all over.

Preheat the oven to 350°.

Put the chicken in a casserole dish, skin-side up, and brush the skin generously with honey. Pour the reserved marinade into the casserol . Cover the chicken with the apple slices, raisins, peaches or apricots (or both), prune slices and grapes. Cover the casserole, and bake the chicken for 45 to 60 minutes, basting frequently.

serves 4

❦ New Orleans Stewed Hen

1 4- to 5-pound stewing hen
1 celery stalk
1 large carrot, cut in half
2 parsley sprigs
1 bay leaf
6 medium-sized onions
hot water
¾ teaspoon salt
¼ teaspoon pepper
3 cups cooked ham, cut in ½-inch cubes
1 pound fresh mushrooms, sliced
⅓ cup butter
2 teaspoons curry powder
2 tablespoons flour
1 cup milk
1 cup heavy cream
½ cup apple cider
3 tablespoons lemon juice

Place the whole hen into a large deep pot. Add the celery, carrot halves, parsley, bay leaf, and 1 onion. Pour enough hot water over the hen to cover it halfway. Bring to a boil. Lower the heat and simmer, covered, for 2 to 2½ hours or until hen is tender. Cool hen in broth.

Remove the hen from the pot. Remove the meat from the bones. Discard the skin and bones. Cut the meat into ½-inch pieces. Strain the chicken broth and place in a saucepan. Cook it over high heat until it is reduced to 2 cups. Set aside.

Chop the remaining onions. In a skillet, melt the butter. To this add the chopped onions, ham and mushrooms. Sauté the mixture until the onions are tender but not brown. Stir in the curry powder and flour. Mix until smooth. Add the reserved broth, milk and cream. Stir until well blended. Continue cooking over low heat for 10 minutes or until the mixture just begins to thicken. Do not let the sauce boil. Add the pieces of hen, salt, pepper, apple cider and lemon juice. Cook 10 minutes longer.

serves 6 to 8

🦐 Southern Fried Chicken

2 3-pound frying chickens, cut into serving
   pieces
2 eggs
1 cup milk
2 teaspoons salt
½ teaspoon black pepper
1 cup flour
shortening or oil for frying
1 tablespoon flour
1 cup light cream, scalded

Rinse and thoroughly dry the chicken pieces.

In a bowl beat the eggs until foamy. Add the milk, salt and pepper. Mix well.

Dip the chicken pieces in the egg mixture. Make sure all the pieces are covered and let them stand in mixture for 10 minutes. Remove the chicken pieces and roll them in the flour. Make sure the pieces are well coated. Shake off the excess flour.

In a deep skillet, heat the shortening or oil to 360° to 365° on a frying thermometer. Place a few pieces of chicken at a time into a frying basket and lower it into the hot shortening. Fry until the pieces are golden brown on all sides, approximately 10 to 15 minutes. As the chicken pieces are cooked, keep them hot until all the pieces are done.

To make the cream gravy, place 2 tablespoons of the shortening the chicken was fried in into a saucepan and heat. Add 1 tablespoon flour and stir until mixture is smooth. Very slowly, add the scalded cream. Stir the mixture constantly until it reaches the boiling point. Remove from heat and season to taste. Serve over the chicken pieces.

serves 6 to 8

🦐 Oven-Fried Chicken

2 2½- to 3-pound chickens cut into serving
   pieces
1 tablespoon salt
1 tablespoon paprika
black pepper to taste
4 tablespoons butter, cut into small pieces

Preheat the oven to 400°.

Rinse the chicken pieces and dry them thoroughly. Season them on all sides with the salt, pepper and paprika.

In a shallow baking pan, place the chicken pieces in one layer. Use more than one pan if needed.

Place 2 tablespoons of the butter pieces evenly over the chicken and cover the pan(s) with aluminum foil. Bake for 20 minutes.

Remove the foil and raise the oven temperature to 450°. Bake 30 minutes longer. Turn the chicken pieces, dot them with the remaining butter, and bake, uncovered, for 30 minutes longer. Remove from oven. Serve hot or cold.

serves 6 to 8

🌿 Key West Lime Chicken

½ cup fresh lime juice
½ teaspoon salt
1 teaspoon ground coriander
1 teaspoon ground cardamom
3 large chicken breasts, halved, skinned and
   boned
olive oil

Combine the lime juice, salt, coriander and cardamom in a mixing bowl. Place the chicken breasts in the bowl and cover with the marinade. Marinate 2 hours.

Remove the chicken breasts from the bowl and reserve the marinade.

Brush each piece of chicken with olive oil and place the pieces in a large skillet. Pour the reserved marinade over the chicken. Simmer, covered, over low heat for 45 minutes or until the chicken is tender.

serves 4

🌿 "Shushed" Eggs

8 eggs
4 teaspoons butter
salt to taste
black pepper to taste

In a heavy skillet, melt the butter and let it brown slightly.

Break the eggs into a bowl and season to taste with salt and pepper. Beat only until the yolks and white are barely mixed. Do not overmix.

Pour the eggs into the brown butter. Stir, cooking only until the eggs are set, about 3 minutes. Serve hot.

serves 4

🌿 Mallard Duck and Turnip Stew

1 mallard duck, jointed and cut into quarters
3 teaspoons vegetable oil
1 tablespoon flour
1 medium-sized onion, finely chopped
2 garlic cloves, finely chopped
salt to taste
black pepper to taste
water
5 medium-sized turnips, peeled and quartered
½ cup coarsely chopped scallions

In a large skillet, heat the oil. Add the duck pieces and sauté until brown on both sides, about 6 to 8 minutes. Remove the duck and set aside.

Add the flour to the oil in the skillet and stir until it forms a dark thick roux, about 3 minutes.

Add the onion, garlic, salt and pepper. Mix well. Return the pieces of duck to the skillet and add enough water to cover them.

Cover the skillet and simmer 1 hour. Add the turnips and scallion greens and simmer until tender, about 35 to 45 minutes.

serves 4

Fish and Seafood

From the Carolina coast down to the Florida Keys, and across the Gulf Coast to New Orleans are some of the best fish and seafood to be found anywhere in the world. Pompano, red snapper, redfish, shrimp, crawfish, rockfish, and oysters...a real bounty of the sea. But it's more than just the fish that makes for great eating—it's the vast array and variety of ingredients, sauces, spices and preparations that give them all a unique Southern flavor.

In this chapter I've gathered some of my favorite recipes—the best of the catch—to share with you that special flavor Southern cooks have given to our fish and seafood. Recipes like the mildly tart and succulent Lemon-Lime Red Snapper, the unusual and delightful taste of Baked Stuffed Shad, the rich, juicy flavor of Southern Smoked Fish, my spicy Shrimp Creole, and the crispy, tender texture of Fried Oysters will delight your family and friends.

It doesn't matter whether you're a beginning cook or can whip up a four-star meal in your sleep—all these recipes will come out fine every time.

Grilled Bass with Herbs

6 large bass fillets
1 cup white wine or dry vermouth
⅓ cup olive oil
1 cup chopped mushrooms
½ cup chopped scallions
2 tablespoons lemon juice
2 teaspoons salt
¼ teaspoon cayenne pepper
¼ teaspoon dried tarragon

Heat the coals in a barbecue until they are gray and very hot.

Cut 6 pieces of heavy aluminum foil (or doubled regular aluminum foil) into 18-inch squares. Lightly oil the foil.

In a large bowl combine the wine or vermouth, olive oil, mushrooms, scallions, lemon juice, salt, cayenne pepper and tarragon. Mix well.

Place one fillet on each piece of foil. Pour the dressing over the fillets. Wrap the fish in the foil and seal tightly. Place the packages on the grill, about 6 inches from the coals.

Grill for 20 to 25 minutes, or until fish flakes easily with a fork. Serve hot.

serves 6

Clam Fritters

2 eggs, separated
2 cups finely chopped fresh or canned clams
1 cup fine breadcrumbs
1 teaspoon salt
½ teaspoon black pepper
1 tablespoon chopped chives
⅓ cup milk
olive oil for frying

In a mixing bowl beat the egg yolks until they are thick. Stir in the clams, breadcrumbs, salt, pepper and chives. Mix well. Add enough milk to form a heavy batter.

In a separate bowl, beat the egg whites until they are stiff but not dry. Fold the whites into the clam batter.

Heat the olive oil in a heavy skillet. Drop the batter by teaspoons into the oil. Fry, turning once, until the fritters are browned on both sides, about 5 to 8 minutes. Serve hot with lemon wedges or tartar sauce.

serves 4

🦐 Soft-Shell Crabs

18 soft-shell crabs
flour
2 tablespoons ground ginger
butter
salt to taste
black pepper to taste

Wash the crabs thoroughly and drain well. Fill a small plastic or paper bag one-quarter full with flour. Add the ginger and mix. Put the crabs in the bag, one at a time, and shake until they are well coated with flour.

Melt enough butter in a skillet to fill it to a depth of ½ inch. Heat the butter until it bubbles. Add as many crabs to the skillet as will fit without the crabs touching each other. Dust the tops of the crabs with salt and pepper and fry until the crabs are golden brown on the bottom. Turn the crabs over, dust again with salt and pepper, and fry until golden brown on the other side. Fry all the crabs in this manner, adding more butter as needed.

Serve the crabs hot, with the butter and drippings spooned over them. Garnish with lemon slices.

serves 6

🦐 Soft-Shell Crabs à lá Créole

12 soft-shell crabs
2 cups milk
4 tablespoons flour
½ cup melted butter
salt to taste
black pepper to taste
2 lemons, quartered
parsley for garnish

Wash the crabs thoroughly and drain well. Season each crab generously with salt and pepper.

Season the milk with salt and pepper. Place the crabs in the milk and soak them for 30 minutes.

Remove the crabs from the milk and dust them lightly with the flour. Brush each crab with melted butter.

Preheat the broiler.

Place the crabs on a rack set in a broiler pan. Broil until the crabs are a delicate brown, about 15 minutes. Turn crabs over after about 7 minutes.

Serve on a platter garnished with lemon quarters and parsley. Pour a little melted butter and chopped parsley over the crabs.

🦐 Fried Oysters

1 quart fresh oysters, shelled and drained
corn meal
4 eggs
¼ teaspoon Tabasco or chili sauce
salt
black pepper
2 tablespoons baking powder
vegetable oil

Spread some corn meal on a plate. On another plate, spread some more corn meal and mix in the baking powder and salt and pepper to taste.

Beat the eggs well in a large bowl. Add the Tabasco or chili sauce and beat again.

Dredge the oysters in the unseasoned corn meal. Dip each oyster into the egg mixture and then into the seasoned corn meal.

Heat the vegetable oil in a deep fryer. Add the oysters, a few at a time, and fry for about 5 minutes, or until they are golden.

serves 4

🦪 Oyster Casserole

1 quart fresh oysters, shelled
2 tablespoons finely chopped parsely
1 small onion, diced
2 tablespoons finely minced shallots
½ teaspoon salt
¼ teaspoon cayenne pepper
1 tablespoon lemon or lime juice
plain soda crackers
3 cups light cream
butter
garlic powder
dry mustard

Grease a casserole dish with butter, and spread a layer of oysters on the bottom. Spread some of the parsley, onion, shallot on top of the oysters, and dust with half the salt and pepper. Sprinkle with half the lemon juice, then make a layer of soda crackers on top of the oysters. Spread another layer of oysters on top of the crackers, and repeat the layering as before.

Preheat the oven to 325°.

Pour the cream over the casserole. Top with thin pats of butter all over the surface. Dust with garlic powder and mustard to taste. Bake for about 30 minutes, or until the cream is thickened and bubbly.

serves 6

🦞 Broiled Crawfish

50 crawfish
4 quarts water
herb bouquet (1 garlic clove, chopped, 1 teaspoon whole allspice, and 6 whole cloves, tied in a square of cheesecloth)
½ gallon white wine or white wine vinegar
3 tablespoons salt
1 teaspoon cayenne pepper

Bring the water to a boil in a very large pot Add the herb bouquet and boil for 3 to 5 minutes. Add the white wine or vinegar and 3 tablespoons salt. Add the cayenne pepper.

Add all the crawfish to the pot. Boil for 20 minutes or until the crawfish are bright red.

Remove the pot from the heat and let the crawfish cool in their liquid.

Serve crawfish piled high on a platter. Accompany with salt, pepper, oil, and spiced vinegar.

Called crayfish everywhere but Gulf Coast kitchens, crawfish are freshwater crustaceans that resemble lobsters but are much smaller.

serves 4 to 6

❧ Pompano à lá Maitre d'Hôtel

4 pounds pompano, either one large fish or several small ones
salt to taste
black pepper to taste
1 tablespoon olive oil
1 tablespoon butter
juice of 1 lemon
1 lemon, sliced
parsley for garnish
Maitre d'hôtel sauce:
1 tablespoon butter
1 tablespoon flour
juice of ½ lemon
1 tablespoon chopped parsley
2 cups fish or chicken broth
1 egg yolk, beaten

Preheat the broiler.

Clean the fish. If the fish are large, split them down the back; if small, broil them whole.

Put the fish in a broiler pan and broil until well browned, about 10 to 12 minutes per side. Turn the fish once.

When done, remove the fish to a heated serving platter and dot them with butter. Sprinkle them with lemon juice. Garnish with the lemon slices and parsley sprigs.

To make the maitre d'hôtel sauce, place the butter and flour in a saucepan. Heat and stir until well blended. Do not burn. Continue mixing over low heat and add the fish or chicken broth. Stir well. Add the lemon juice and chopped parsley. Bring the sauce to a boil and let it boil for about 15 minutes. Remove the saucepan from the heat and stir in the egg yolk. Mix until well blended. Serve with the broiled fish.

serves 4

❧ Deep-Fried Porgy

3 pounds porgy or butterfish, filleted but not skinned
2 teaspoons salt
½ teaspoon black pepper
½ cup yellow cornmeal
lard or oil for deep frying

Score the fillets on the fleshy side with a sharp knife, making approximately 3 small slashes per fillet.

Season the fillets well with salt and pepper on both sides. Dip them into the corn meal, making sure the fillets are coated evenly. Shake off any excess corn meal.

In a large deep skillet heat a ½-inch layer of oil or lard. When very hot add the fish. Fry for 4 minutes on the first side. Turn the fillets carefully and fry for 3 to 4 minutes longer or until fish is golden brown. Drain the fish on paper towels and serve hot.

serves 4

❧ Baked Redfish

1 4-pound redfish
3 to 4 tablespoons butter
salt to taste
cayenne pepper to taste
6 cooked shrimps, shelled, deveined and coarsely chopped
¼ cup chopped capers
lemon wedges for garnish

Preheat the oven to 400°.

Place 2 tablespoons of the butter, cut up into small pieces, inside the fish. Dot the outside of the fish with the remaining butter. Season the fish with salt and cayenne pepper.

Place the fish in a well-buttered shallow baking dish. Cover with a piece of well-buttered brown paper cut to fit. Bake for 40 minutes, or until the fish flakes easily with a fork.

Five minutes before the fish is ready, remove it from the oven. Sprinkle the capers and shrimp around the fish. Return to the oven for 5 minutes. Serve garnished with lemon wedges.

serves 4 to 5

Rockfish

1 3-pound rockfish
salt to taste
black pepper to taste
flour
6 thick bacon strips
1 large onion, diced
½ cup chopped scallion
3 tablespoons brandy
1 cup water

Preheat the oven to 350°.

Make three ½-inch-deep cuts in each side of the fish. Sprinkle the fish with salt, pepper and flour on both sides. Wrap the bacon strips around the fish.

Put the fish in a shallow baking dish. Sprinkle the onions and scallions on top of the fish. Pour the water and brandy into the baking dish and cover. Bake for 20 minutes, then remove the cover and continue to bake until the fish is well browned. Serve with Worcestershire sauce.

serves 4

Baked Stuffed Shad

1 large shad, at least 4 pounds, with roe
3 tablespoons lemon juice
2 cups water
4 scallions, finely chopped
¼ cup vegetable oil
2 eggs, beaten
1 cup unseasoned breadcrumbs
½ cup water
½ teaspoon dried basil
½ cup lemon juice
2 tablespoons Worcestershire sauce
1 dash Angostura or Peychaud's bitters

Remove the roe from the fish. Put the water into a pot and bring it to a boil. Add the 3 tablespoons of lemon juice. Gently add the roe and cook it until it is firm, about 3 to 5 minutes. Remove the membrane from the roe.

Heat the vegetable oil in a skillet. Add the chopped scallions and sauté until tender. Add the roe, eggs and breadcrumbs. Stir all the ingredients together. Add the water, a little at a time, moistening the stuffing until it is the way you like it. Fold in the basil and season with salt and pepper to taste.

Preheat the oven to 325°.

Stuff the shad with the roe stuffing and close the cavity with toothpicks or poultry skewers. Place the shad in a moderately deep baking dish, and add enough cold water to fill the dish to a depth of 1 inch. Pour the Worcestershire sauce and bitters over the fish.

Bake for 40 minutes, basting every 5 minutes to keep the shad moist.

serves 6

🎔 Shrimp Creole

2 tablespoons butter
2 tablespoons flour
1 cup chopped onion
1/3 cup chopped green pepper
2 garlic cloves, chopped
3 cups canned tomatoes, with their liquid
1 pound fresh okra, sliced
2 bay leaves
salt to taste
black pepper to taste
1/2 teaspoon Tabasco sauce
2 pounds uncooked shrimp, peeled and deveined

Melt the butter in a large skillet. Stir in the flour and cook over low heat, stirring constantly, until the flour is a medium brown color. Add the onion, green pepper and garlic. Cook, stirring occasionally, until the onion is soft, about 5 to 8 minutes. Stir in the tomatoes, okra, bay leaves, salt, pepper and Tabasco sauce. Bring the mixture to a boil and then lower the heat. Cover the skillet and simmer for 30 minutes, stirring frequently.

Add the shrimp and cook for 10 minutes longer. If the mixture is too thick, thin it with a little hot water. Serve with rice.

serves 4 to 6

🎔 Shrimp in Beer

2 pounds uncooked shrimp, unshelled
3 cups beer
2 garlic cloves, chopoped
1 teaspoon salt
1/2 teaspoon dried thyme
1 teaspoon celery seeds
1 tablespoon finely chopped parsley
1/2 teaspoon Tabasco sauce
2 tablespoons lemon juice
melted butter

In a saucepan combine the shrimp, beer, garlic, salt, thyme, parsley and Tabasco sauce. Bring the mixture to a boil. Lower the heat and simmer for 4 minutes, or until the shrimp are pink.

Drain the shrimp and serve with melted butter.

serves 4

🎔 Creole Boiled Shrimp

100 uncooked shrimp
3 tablespoons salt
1 large head celery, with leaves, coarsely chopped
1 teaspoon whole allspice
1/2 teaspoon whole mace
6 whole cloves
4 parsley sprigs
4 bay leaves
1/2 teaspoon dried thyme
1 dried hot red pepper pod
salt to taste
black pepper to taste
cayenne pepper to taste

Fill a very large pot with water and add the 3 tablespoons salt. Add the celery, allspice, mace, cloves, thyme, parsley, bay leaves, cayenne pepper and red pepper pod. Bring the water to a boil. Allow the water to boil for 3 minutes.

Drop all the shrimp into the pot. Boil for 10 minutes and then remove the pot from the heat. Set aside and cool the shrimp in the cooking liquid. Drain and serve at room temperature.

serves 6 to 8

🌿 Marinated Broiled Shrimp

½ cup olive oil
2 teaspoons ground turmeric
2 garlic cloves, crushed
½ teaspoon black pepper
2 teaspoons chili powder
2 tablespoons red wine vinegar
3 teaspoons dried basil
2 pounds uncooked shrimp, peeled and deveined

In a mixing bowl combine the olive oil, turmeric, garlic, pepper, chili powder, wine vinegar and basil. Add the shrimp to the bowl and mix well. Cover and let stand at room temperature for 3 hours.

Preheat the broiler.

Place the shrimp in a broiling pan and broil for 10 minutes. Baste often with the marinade. Serve hot.

serves 6

🌿 Lemon-Lime Red Snapper

½ cup finely chopped scallions
¼ cup lime juice
2 teaspoons grated lemon peel
1 teaspoon salt
4 red snapper fillets, unskinned
¼ teaspoon grated nutmeg
black pepper to taste

In a shallow baking dish, combine the scallions, lime juice, lemon peel and salt. Mix well.

Add the fillets to the baking dish and turn them to coat with the marinade. The fillets should fit in one layer. Place the fillets skin-side up and marinate for 30 minutes at room temperature.

Preheat the oven to 400°.

Turn the fillets skin-side down. Sprinkle them with nutmeg and pepper. Bake the fish for 10 to 12 minutes or until it flakes easily with a fork. Baste frequently. Serve hot from the baking dish.

serves 4

🌿 Red Snapper with Chili Pepper

4 red snapper fillets
2 tablespoons olive oil
1 garlic clove, chopped
½ cup chopped onion
½ cup sliced pimiento-stuffed green olives
¼ cup chopped sweet red pepper
1 teaspoon chopped coriander
1 dried hot red chili pepper, seeded and crushed
6 tablespoons lemon juice
6 tablespoons orange juice
½ teaspoon salt
¼ teaspoon black pepper

Preheat the oven to 375°.

Wash and dry the fillets. Place them in a lightly buttered shallow baking dish.

In a skillet, heat the olive oil. Add the garlic and onion and sauté until the onion is soft. Add the olives, sweet red pepper, coriander and crushed chili pepper. Stir constantly and cook for 3 minutes. Add the orange juice, lemon juice, salt and pepper. Stir until well blended.

Pour the mixture over the fillets and bake, uncovered, for 15 to 20 minutes or until the fish flakes easily.

Serve on a platter with the pan juices poured over the fish.

serves 4

🌿 Red Snapper Gulf-Style

2 pounds red snapper fillets
salt and pepper to taste
black pepper to taste
2 tablespoons softened butter
½ cup chopped carrot
1 celery stalk, chopped
2 tablespoons chopped parsley
6 uncooked shrimp, peeled and chopped
1 cup white wine or dry vermouth
¼ teaspoon dried basil

Preheat the oven to 400°.

Pat the fillets dry. Rub them with salt and pepper and place them into a heavily buttered deep casserole or baking dish.

In a bowl, combine the butter, carrots, celery, parsley, shrimp, white wine and basil. Mix well. Pour the sauce over the fish.

Bake the fish for 30 minutes or until it flakes easily. Serve hot in the baking dish.

serves 4

🌿 Brook Trout with Seafood Sauce

2 onions, diced
butter
6 trout fillets, about ½ pound each
salt to taste
black pepper to taste
paprika
½ cup lemon juice
6 tablespoons butter
2 tablespoons flour
9 large cooked shrimp, shelled, deveined and chopped
4 large black olives, chopped
6 large white mushrooms, coarsely chopped
1 dozen small oysters, shelled
½ cup dry white wine
grated Cheddar cheese

Preheat the oven to 350°.

Grease a baking dish with some butter, and spread the onion on the bottom. Lay the trout fillets side by side on top of the onions. Season them with salt, pepper and a dusting of paprika. Spoon ¼ cup of the lemon juice over each fillet. Bake the fillets for 25 minutes.

While the fillets are baking, prepare the sauce. Melt the butter in a skillet over low heat. Slowly blend in the flour. Slowly stir in the remaining lemon juice, then add the shrimp, olives, mushrooms, oysters and wine. Simmer the sauce in the skillet until the shrimp and oysters are opaque and the mushrooms are soft and tender, about 8 to 12 minutes.

When fillets have cooked for 25 minutes, remove the baking dish from the oven. With a spatula, remove four of the fillets. Arrange the remaining fillets in the center of the dish so that they overlap slightly. Spoon some of the seafood sauce over the two fillets. Use the spatula to lay two more fillets on top, being careful not to break the fillets. Spoon on more sauce, and repeat again with last two fillets and the remainder of the sauce.

Sprinkle the fish with the grated cheese and dust with a little paprika for color. Return the dish to the oven and bake for another 10 to 12 minutes, or until the cheese has melted and the sauce is piping hot. Serve in the baking dish.

serves 6

🦐 Catfish Fry

2 pounds catfish fillets
1 egg
2 tablespoons water
½ cup flour
½ cup corn meal
1 teaspoon salt
⅛ teaspoon black pepper
½ cup olive oil

Wash and pat dry the fillets. If the fillets are very large, cut them into smaller pieces.

In a shallow dish, beat the egg slightly. Stir in the water and set the dish aside.

In another shallow dish combine the flour, corn meal, salt and pepper.

Dip the catfish fillets in the egg and coat well. Then dip the fillets in the flour mixture and coat well. Shake off excess.

Heat the oil in a skillet. Add the fish and brown on both sides. Cook until the fish flakes easily, approximately 10 to 12 minutes.

Drain on paper towels. Serve hot with tartar sauce or lemon wedges.

serves 4

🦐 Oven-Fried Catfish

2 pounds catfish fillets
1 cup dry sherry
1 tablespoon salt
1 cup unflavored breadcrumbs
⅓ cup vegetable oil
2 lemons, sliced

Preheat the oven to 450°.

Wash and pat dry the fillets. If the fillets are very large, cut them into smaller pieces.

Place the breadcrumbs in a baking dish and toast in the oven for 1 minute. Remove and mix with salt.

Dip the fillets, one at a time, into the sherry and then into the breadcrumbs. Coat evenly with the crumbs.

Place the fillets onto a well-oiled baking sheet. Sprinkle the fish with the remaining oil and sherry. Bake for 15 minutes. Serve with lemon slices.

serves 6

🦐 Fried Catfish

2 pounds catfish fillets
salt to taste
black pepper to taste
¼ cup bacon drippings
juice of 1 lemon
¼ cup chopped parsley

Wash and pat dry the fillets. If the fillets are very large, cut them into smaller pieces. Season the fish well with salt and pepper.

In a large skillet heat the bacon drippings. When hot, add the fish. Cook over moderate heat until the fillets are golden brown, about 12 to 15 minutes. Turn once while cooking.

Drain the fish on paper towels. Sprinkle with lemon juice and parsley. Serve hot.

serves 4

🦐 Saucy Creole Fish

4 tablespoons butter
2 tablespoons chopped onion
4 tablespoons chopped celery
2 tablespoons chopped sweet red pepper
2 tablespoons flour
½ cup light cream
½ cup fine breadcrumbs
¼ teaspoon dried rosemary
1 cup cooked crabmeat
1 cup coarsely chopped cooked shrimp
¼ cup chopped parsley
¼ teaspoon salt
¼ teaspoon black pepper
1½ teaspoons Worcestershire sauce
½ teaspoon Tabasco sauce
6 fillets of sole or flounder
3 tablespoons melted butter

Creole sauce ingredients:
4 cups canned tomatoes
2 tablespoons butter
2 garlic cloves, chopped
1 bay leaf
1 teaspoon salt
¼ teaspoon black pepper
⅛ teaspoon cayenne pepper
1 tablespoon flour

Preheat the oven to 350°.

In a saucepan melt the butter. Add the onion, celery and red pepper. Cook until tender, about 5 to 8 minutes. Carefully stir in the flour and stir until the mixture is smooth. Add the light cream and continue cooking until the mixture has thickened.

Remove the saucepan from the heat. Stir in the breadcrumbs, rosemary, crabmeat, shrimp, parsley, salt, pepper, Worcestershire sauce and Tabasco. Cook until all the ingredients are hot.

Place the 6 fillets flat on a work surface. Place a heaping tablespoon of the filling on each fillet. Roll up the fillets and secure them with toothpicks.

Place the fillets about 1 to 2 inches apart in a baking dish. Brush the fillets with the melted butter and sprinkle them with salt. Bake the fillets for 15 minutes. Pour the Creole sauce over the fillets, reduce the oven temperature to 325° and bake 30 minutes longer.

To prepare the Creole sauce, combine the tomatoes, half the butter, garlic, bay leaf, salt, pepper and cayenne in a saucepan. Cook over moderate heat, stirring occasionally, until the mixture is reduced by half, about 20 to 30 minutes.

In a small saucepan, melt the remaining butter. Stir in the flour and continue cooking until the flour is lightly browned.

Add the flour mixture to the tomato mixture and cook for 2 to 3 minutes. Remove the sauce from the heat and strain it through a sieve. Pour the sauce over the fish and continue baking.

serves 6

Watermelon Rind Pickles

Shrimp and Bean Salad

Lemon-Lime Red Snapper

Hominy Grits

Manor House Apple Salad

French Chicken

🌿 Gumbos and Stews 🌿

You may not taste it when you serve these gumbos and stews, but mixed in with all the ingredients and spices is always a little bit of history…the flavor of times gone by. Most gumbo recipes have been cooking up in Southern kitchens for hundreds of years now. They've been passed down from mother to daughter, friend to friend, neighbor to neighbor—each of them changing a little here, adding a little something special there, a new dash, a different touch, so that today nobody really knows where and who the original recipes came from.

Good Southern cooks treat their gumbo and stew recipes like fine family heirlooms. They bring out their best only for special people and special occasions. If one of them shares her recipe with you, it means she values you as the very best of friends.

So I suppose you could say these recipes are the jewels of Southern cooking, using ingredients that are diamonds in the rough waiting to be turned into precious gems like Mardi Gras Seafood Gumbo, Kentucky Burgoo, Plantation Chicken and Vegetable Stew, Old Creole Vegetable Gumbo, Creole Veal Stew, and my personal favorite, Gumbo Filé.

🌿 Brunswick Stew

2 3-pound chickens, cut into serving pieces
2 pounds boneless shoulder of veal, in 1 piece
1 ham bone
3 quarts water
½ cup sugar
1 bay leaf
1 teaspoon dried basil
1 tablespoon chopped fresh parsley
2 onions, sliced
4 cups tomatoes, peeled and chopped
4 celery stalks with leaves, chopped
2 cups fresh lima beans
4 cups fresh corn, cut from the cob
½ cup butter
1 teaspoon crushed hot red pepper flakes
4 medium-sized potatoes, peeled, cooked and
    mashed

In a large pot combine the chicken, veal, ham bone, water, sugar, bay leaf, basil and parsley. Cook over low heat until the veal and chicken are very tender, about 50 minutes.

Remove the veal and chicken pieces from the broth and set aside.

Add the onions, tomatoes, celery and lima beans to the broth. Cook over low heat until the beans are tender, about 15 minutes. Stir often.

Cut the veal into small pieces. Remove the chicken from the bones and cut into small pieces. Discard the bones and skin.

Return the veal and chicken meat to the pot. Add the corn and simmer the stew for 10 minutes.

Stir in the butter, red pepper flakes and pepper. Season to taste with salt.

Stir the mashed potatoes into the stew. Cook, stirring constantly, for 15 minutes or until the stew thickens and the potatoes are absorbed. Serve hot.

The original recipe for Brunswick Stew called for squirrel instead of chicken. Brunswick County, North Carolina, and Brunswick County, Virginia still argue about which originated the stew.

serves 8

🌿 Charleston Oyster Stew with Sesame Seeds

4 tablespoons sesame seeds
2 onions, thinly sliced
6 strips bacon or salt pork
3 tablespoons flour
2 cups oyster liquor or 1 cup water and 1 cup dry sherry
3 cups shelled oysters

Preheat the oven to 450°.

Spread the sesame seeds (also called benne seeds) on a foil-covered baking sheet. Toast the seeds in the oven until they are browned. Set aside.

Fry the bacon and onion in a heavy stew pot until the bacon is cooked but not crisp. Remove the bacon and onion and set aside. Leave the drippings in the pot.

Reduce the heat a little and slowly stir in the flour, continuing to stir until the drippings become a rich brown gravy. Gradually stir in the oyster liquor until it is thoroughly blended. Simmer the mixture over medium heat, stirring constantly for about 5 minutes, or until the mixture has thickened and is very smooth.

Put the reserved sesame seeds into a small plastic bag. Seal the bag and crush the seeds with a rolling pin until they are a coarse powder. Add the powder to the stew and stir well.

Chop the reserved bacon strips into small pieces, and add them and the reserved onion to the stew. Add the oysters and cook about 5 to 10 minutes, or until the edges of the oysters curl.

Serve piping hot over hominy.

serves 8

🌿 Kentucky Burgoo

2½ tablespoons lard or olive oil
1 pound lean beef shank
1 pound beef bones
½ pound veal shoulder
1 3-pound chicken, quartered
2 quarts water
1½ teaspoons salt
2 cups chopped onions
1 garlic clove, chopped
1 cup peeled and diced potatoes
4 celery stalks with leaves, diced
1 20-ounce can tomatoes
3 carrots, peeled and diced
1 large green pepper, chopped
1 cup fresh butter or waxed beans
½ teaspoon crushed hot red pepper flakes
1 small onion
1 bay leaf
⅛ cup dark brown sugar
¼ teaspoon black pepper
1 cup sliced fresh okra
1½ cups fresh corn, cut from the cob
¼ cup butter
½ cup flour
½ cup finely chopped parsley

In a large pot heat half the lard or oil. Add the beef shank, beef bones and veal. Brown for about 8 minutes.

Add the chicken, water and salt. Cover the pot and cook over low heat until the meat is very tender, about 30 to 40 minutes.

Remove the meat and chicken. When cool enough to handle, remove the meat from the bones. Cut it into small pieces and return it to the pot. Discard the bones and chicken skin.

In a skillet, sauté the onions in the remaining lard or oil until soft but not brown, about 5 minutes. Add the onions to the pot. Stir in the garlic, potatoes, celery, tomatoes, carrots, green pepper, beans, red pepper flakes, onion, bay leaf, brown sugar and pepper. Cook over low heat for 2 hours, stirring occasionally.

Add the okra and corn. Cook for 15 minutes longer.

In a small bowl, blend together the butter and flour. Add the burgoo and cook, stirring constantly, until the mixture thickens. Season the burgoo to taste and sprinkle it with chopped parsley before serving.

Although burgoo originated as a sort of thick porridge on board sailing vessels in the mid-1800s, it came to mean a thick meat stew as made in Kentucky. Burgoo is made in huge quantities for large events like Fourth of July picnics and Derby Day.

serves 8 to 10

Louisiana Crab Stew

2 tablespoons butter
1 small onion, chopped
2 cups thinly sliced mushrooms
2 tomatoes, peeled and chopped
1 pound crabmeat, cooked and flaked
1 teaspoon salt
1/8 teaspoon cayenne pepper
1 cup heavy cream
1/2 cup light cream
2 tablespoons chopped parsley
1 teaspoon chopped chives
1/4 cup brandy

Melt the butter in a large skillet over moderate heat. Add the onion and cook for 2 minutes. Add the mushrooms and continue cooking for 2 to 3 minutes. Add the tomatoes, stir and cook for 5 minutes. Add the crabmeat, salt, cayenne pepper, heavy cream and light cream. Continue to cook until the mixture just comes to a boil. Immediately remove the skillet from the heat. Stir in the parsley, chives and brandy. Serve hot with rice.

serves 4

Plantation Chicken and Vegetable Stew

1 4-pound roasting chicken, cut into stew-sized pieces
3 tablespoons vegetable oil
1½ cups water
½ cup sherry
1 tablespoon salt
½ teaspoon white pepper
10 white onions, halved
1 cup fresh green peas
1 cup sliced peeled carrots
½ cup diced peeled turnip
1 cup diced peeled potatoes
½ cup corn
1/3 cup flour
½ cup warm water
chopped parsley

Heat the vegetable oil in a Dutch oven or large heavy pot. Add the chicken pieces and brown them on all sides. Add the water, sherry, salt and pepper. Cover and simmer over medium heat for 45 minutes.

Add the onions, green peas, carrots, turnip, potatoes and corn to the stew. Cover and simmer for another 40 minutes.

Combine the flour and warm water in a bowl. Stir the mixture into the stew. Continue to cook for another 5 to 8 minutes, or until the stew thickens. Serve over rice.

serves 6

❧ Gumbo Filé

1 5-pound chicken, cut into serving pieces
2 teaspoons salt
1 teaspoon black pepper
1 garlic clove, chopped
3 tablespoons butter
2 medium-sized onions, chopped
½ pound boiled ham, cut into strips
3 quarts water
½ teaspoon dried thyme
½ teaspoon dried rosemary
¼ teaspoon chili powder
1 cup canned tomatoes
1 cup sliced fresh okra
24 oysters, shelled
1 tablespoon filé powder

Rub the salt, pepper and garlic pieces into the chicken.

In a large saucepan, melt the butter. Add the onions and the chicken and cook until the chicken pieces are lightly browned, about 8 minutes. Add the ham, water, thyme, rosemary, chili powder and tomatoes. Cover and simmer for 2½ hours.

Add the okra and cook 1 hour longer.

Add the oysters. Bring the mixture to a boil and cook for 3 minutes.

Remove the saucepan from heat and stir in filé powder. Mix well. Do not allow the gumbo to boil. Do not reheat the gumbo after the filé powder has been added or the gumbo will become stringy. Serve hot in soup bowls.

❧ Mardi Gras Seafood Gumbo

¼ cup bacon drippings
3 pounds thinly sliced fresh okra
¼ cup vegetable oil
¼ cup flour
4 onions, diced
2 tablespoons tomato paste
¼ cup puréed tomatoes
4 cups cold water
½ pound oysters, shelled
1 pound crabmeta, picked and flaked
2 pounds medium-sized shrimp, shelled and deveined
¾ pound diced baked ham
3 bay leaves
½ cup chopped parsley
2 garlic cloves, minced
1 shallot, chopped
salt to taste
black pepper to taste
1 teaspoon chili sauce

Heat the bacon drippings in a skillet over low heat. Add the okra and sauté until the mixture thickens. Remove the skillet from the heat and set aside.

In a heavy stew pot or Dutch oven, heat the vegetable oil. Slowly blend in the flour, stirring constantly until a rich, brown gravy (roux) is formed.

Add the onions, tomato paste, puréed tomatoes and water and mix thoroughly. Then add the reserved okra and drippings, and the oysters, crabmeat, shrimp, ham, bay leaves, parsley, garlic, shallot, salt and pepper. Mix well.

Simmer the gumbo over medium heat for 45 minutes to 1 hour, or until the seafood is tender and opaque. Stir in the chili sauce just before removing the gumbo from the heat. Serve piping hot over saffron rice.

serves 10

🌿 Vegetables and Side Dishes 🌿

You're probably familiar with the expression "a sit-down dinner with all the fixin's." Well, these are the "fixin's." The dishes in this chapter are the ones that make the meal unmistakably Southern.

Down where I live, when people get to talking about last night's dinner, you hear them say things like "a fine Smithfield ham with sweet potatoes" or "a big, bubblin' chicken pie with some of that good corn pudding." It's always that way—the vegetables or side dishes mentioned in the same breath with the main course because most people just can't picture one without the other. In fact, some vegetable dishes were created specifically for a particular main course. Like Stuffed Acorn Squash with Southern fried chicken; Sweet Potato Pone with baked glazed ham; or Country Green Beans with smoked Southern fish. These are delicious, but the real joy in cooking and eating these dishes is discovering your own combinations. Finding just the perfect accompaniment for your best meat, poultry or fish recipe is the best way to start your family and friends talking about the "fine chicken and Down-Home Carrot Casserole" or the "tasty fish dinner with Creole-style stewed okra" you cooked up last night. Believe me, this can be the nicest kind of fame you can get.

🌿 Red Beans and Rice

1 pound dried red kidney beans
2 small ham hocks
2 tablespoons vegetable oil
1 tablespoon finely chopped garlic
2 cups finely chopped onions
1 cup finely chopped green peppers
1 cup finely chopped celery
¼ cup finely chopped parsley
¼ teaspoon cayenne pepper
1 bay leaf
½ teaspoon dried thyme
1 teaspoon Tabasco sauce
1 teaspoon sugar
salt to taste
black pepper to taste
1 cup chopped canned tomatoes
1 pound smoked sausage, cut into thick slices
1 cup finely chopped scallions

Put the beans and ham hocks in a large bowl. Add 8 cups cold water and soak the beans and ham hocks overnight.

Drain the beans and ham hocks and put them into a large heavy pot or Dutch oven. Add 8 cups cold water and bring the liquid to a boil over moderate heat.

Heat the oil in a skillet and add the garlic, onions, green peppers and celery. Sauté, stirring often, for 3 minutes. Add the mixture to the beans. Add the parsley, cayenne pepper, bay leaf, thyme, Tabasco sauce, sugar, salt, black pepper and tomatoes to the beans. stir well. Cook the beans, uncovered, over moderate heat for 2 hours, add the sausage slices.

Just before the beans are ready to serve, remove 1 cup of beans, with cooking liquid, from the pot. Purée the removed beans in a blender or food processor and return the purée to the pot. Stir well.

Serve the beans over rice in deep soup bowls. Garnish each serving with chopped scallions.

serves 8 to 10

❧ Cowboy Beans

2 cups dried pinto beans
1 ham bone
1 hot red pepper pod
1 teaspoon salt
¼ pound salt pork, chopped
1 large onion, chopped
1 garlic clove, chopped
4 tomatoes, chopped
½ teaspoon ground cumin
1½ tablespoons chili powder
1 teaspoon salt

Rinse the dried beans well under cold running water. Place beans in a large pot with 6 cups cold water. Soak overnight.

In the morning add the ham bone, red chili pepper, and salt to the undrained beans. Bring the mixture to a boil. Reduce the heat and cover. Simmer gently until the beans are tender, about 3 to 4 hours. Drain and reserve 1 cup of the liquid.

When the beans are almost done, heat the salt pork in a large skillet. Stir in the onion and garlic and cook for 5 minutes. Add the tomatoes, reserved bean liquid, cumin, chili powder and salt. Mix well. Cook over low heat, stirring frequently, for 45 minutes.

Mix in the beans and continue to simmer for 20 minutes longer. Remove from heat and serve.

serves 6

❧ Boiled Pinto Beans

2 cups dried pinto beans
12 cups water
1 medium-sized onion
2 garlic cloves, crushed
1 teaspoon salt
¼ teaspoon sugar

Rinse the dried beans well under cold running water. Place them in a large bowl with 6 cups cold water and soak overnight.

Drain the soaked beans and place them in a large saucepan. Add 6 cups water, the onion and garlic. Bring the water to a boil over high heat. Reduce the heat and simmer 3½ to 4 hours, partially covered.

Add the salt and sugar. Continue to simmer 30 minutes longer or until the beans are tender but still intact. Drain the beans and serve hot.

serves 8

❧ Hoppin' John

1 cup dried blackeyed peas or cowpeas
1 teaspoon salt
1 medium-sized onion, diced
2 ounces diced salt pork
¼ teaspoon black pepper
⅛ teaspoon cayenne pepper
1 cup raw long-grain rice
1 tablespoon butter

Rinse the blackeyed peas well. Put the peas in a bowl with 3 cups of cold water and soak for 8 hours or overnight. Drain well.

Place the blackeyed peas, salt, onion, and salt pork into a large pot. Add 3 cups cold water. Cover the pot and bring the mixture to a boil. Lower the heat and simmer for 1¼ hours, or until the peas are tender. There should be very little water left in the pot. Season with pepper and cayenne.

Bring 1½ cups of water to a boil in a saucepan. Add the rice, lower the heat, and cook, covered, for 18 minutes or until the water is absorbed. Add the butter and toss.

Add the rice to the blackeyed peas and cook for 2 to 3 minutes to blend the flavors. Serve hot.

serves 6 to 8

❧ Down-Home Carrot Casserole

²⁄₃ cup raw long-grain rice
2 cups milk
1 cup water
4 eggs
3 tablespoons sugar
1¼ teaspoons salt
¼ cup chopped pecans
3 cups coarsely shredded carrots
butter

In the top of a double boiler, combine the rice, milk, and water. Cook, covered, over boiling water for 35 minutes or until the rice is tender. Drain any liquid that is left.

Preheat the oven to 350°.

In a mixing bowl beat the eggs. Add the sugar and salt and continue beating until the mixture is light and fluffy. Stir in the cooked rice, chopped pecans and shredded carrots. Mix well.

Butter a 1½-quart baking dish. Put the carrot mixture in the dish and dot with butter. Bake for 1 hour. Serve hot.

serves 6

❧ Minted Carrots

8 to 10 medium-sized carrots, peeled
1 cup water
½ teaspoon salt
3 tablespoons butter, cut into small pieces
black pepper to taste
2 tablespoons coarsely chopped fresh mint leaves,
    or 1 teaspoon crumbled dried mint leaves

Cut the carrots on the diagonal into ¼-inch slices.

In a saucepan combine the water, carrots and salt. Cover and bring the liquid to a boil. Lower the heat and cook for 15 minutes or until the carrots are tender. Drain well and put the carrots into a serving dish. Add the butter and pepper to taste. Add the mint and toss well. Serve hot.

serves 4

❧ Collard Greens

2 pounds fresh collard greens or kale
½ pound chopped salt pork
4 medium-sized potatoes, peeled
salt to taste
black pepper to taste

Wash the collard greens thoroughly. Cut off and discard any tough stems and discolored leaves.

In a very large pot, combine the salt pork and 4 quarts water. Bring the liquid to a boil and cook for 20 minutes. Add the collard greens. Cover the pot and simmer for 1 hour. Add the potatoes and cook for 30 minutes longer or until the potatoes are tender. Drain well. Season to taste with salt and pepper. Serve hot.

serves 6

❧ New Year's Blackeyed Peas in Dressing

1 pound dried blackeyed peas or cowpeas
4 ounces diced salt pork
2 red onions, diced
3 garlic cloves, crushed
2 teaspoons hot red pepper flakes
1 cup peanut oil
1 cup cider vinegar
1 tablespoon Worcestershire sauce
¼ cup brown sugar
1 teaspoon dried basil
pimento-stuffed green olives

Rinse the blackeyed peas well. Put the peas in a large bowl with 6 cups of cold water and soak for 8 hours or overnight. Drain well.

Put the peas into a large pot and add the salt pork. Add 3 quarts of cold water, cover the pot and cook over moderate heat for 1¼ hours or until the peas are tender. Drain well.

In a large, deep bowl, toss the peas, onions, garlic and red pepper flakes together.

Mix the oil, vinegar, Worcestershire sauce, brown sugar and basil in a bowl. Blend well.

Pour the dressing over the peas, cover the bowl and marinate in the refrigerator for a day before serving.

Serve cold, topped with slices of Spanish olives.

serves 8

❧ Corn Oysters

3 cups corn, cut from the cob
3 eggs, well beaten
1½ teaspoons baking powder
½ teaspoon salt
¼ teaspoon black pepper
3 tablespoons light cream
⅓ cup flour
butter

In a large bowl combine the corn, eggs, baking powder, salt, pepper, cream and flour. Beat the mixture until well blended.

Melt 1 tablespoon butter on a griddle. Drop the corn mixture by rounded tablespoons onto the griddle. Fry until the oysters are golden brown on both sides, about 3 to 4 minutes a side. Fry only as many corn oysters as will fit easily on the griddle at one time. Add more butter as needed. Serve hot.

serves 6

❧ Corn Bake

1 tablespoon olive oil
1 onion, finely chopped
2 cups canned tomato purée
2 tablespoons diced celery
2 tablespoons chili powder
2 tablespoons butter
3 cups fresh corn, cut from the cob
    (approximately 4 ears)
1 teaspoon salt
½ teaspoon black pepper

Heat the olive oil in a heavy skillet. Add the onion and sauté until golden, about 5 to 8 minutes. Add the tomato purée, celery, chili powder, butter, corn, salt and pepper. Mix well and remove from heat.

Butter a 1-quart casserole dish. Pour in the corn mixture and bake, uncovered, for 30 minutes. Serve hot from the dish.

serves 6

Fried Corn

3 cups fresh corn, cut from the cob
½ cup boiling water
⅓ cup milk
2 tablespoons bacon drippings
1 teaspoon salt
½ teaspoon sugar
¼ teaspoon black pepper
1 tablespoon flour
2 tablespoons cold water
1 teaspoon butter

In a saucepan combine the boiling water, milk, bacon drippings, salt, sugar and pepper. Add the corn and stir. Bring the mixture to a boil over low heat. When the mixture begins to boil, cover and cook for 10 minutes, or until the corn is tender. Stir occasionally.

In a small bowl combine the flour and the water. Blend until smooth. Add to the corn mixture. Stir and cook 1 minute longer or until the corn begins to thicken. Remove from the heat. Stir in the butter and serve.

This popular dish, which is actually stewed, is misleadingly called fried corn throughout the South.

serves 4

Corn and Okra Mix

4 strips bacon
1 onion, finely chopped
1 cup fresh okra, thinly sliced
3 cups fresh corn, cut from the cob
3 large tomatoes, peeled and diced
1 teaspoon sugar
salt to taste
black pepper to taste
¼ teaspoon Tabasco sauce

Fry the bacon in a large skillet until it is crisp and brown. Drain on paper towels, crumble and reserve. Discard all but 4 table-spoons of the bacon drippings.

Add the corn, okra and onion to the hot bacon drippings. Sauté for 10 minutes, stirring constantly. Add the tomatoes, sugar, salt, pepper and Tabasco sauce. Cover the skillet and simmer over low heat for 25 minutes, stirring occasionally.

Remove the skillet from the heat. Season to taste with additional salt and pepper and sprinkle with the crumbled bacon.

serves 4 to 6

Country Green Beans

1½ pounds fresh green beans, trimmed and
    halved
¼ pound salt pork
1 teaspoon salt
½ teaspoon sugar
boiling water

Place the beans in a large saucepan.

Cut 3 slashes in the salt pork with a sharp knife. Add the salt pork to the beans. Add the salt, sugar and enough boiling water to cover. Cover the saucepan and cook over very low heat for 2 to 3 hours or until all the water has cooked away. Serve hot.

serves 6

✲ Fried Grits

5 cups water
1 teaspoon salt
1 cup regular white hominy grits
1 tablespoon butter
2 eggs, beaten
1 cup unflavored breadcrumbs or flour
4 tablespoons bacon drippings or butter

In a heavy saucepan bring the water and salt to a boil. Slowly stir in the grits. Stir constantly to make a smooth mixture. Lower the heat and cover the saucepan. Cook for 25 to 35 minutes, stirring occasionally. Stir in the butter.

Heavily butter a 9 × 13-inch loaf pan.

Pour the cooked grits into the loaf pan. Let the grits cool and cover the pan with plastic wrap. Refrigerate for 6 hours or overnight.

Carefully unmold the chilled grits loaf and cut it into 12 slices. Dip the slices into the beaten eggs and then the breadcrumbs.

Heat the bacon drippings in a skillet. Add the grits and fry until golden brown, about 3 minutes on each side. Turn carefully. Drain the grits on paper towels. Serve hot with maple syrup.

serves 4 to 6

✲ Grits and Cheese Casserole

5 cups water
1 teaspoon salt
1 cup regular white hominy grits
½ cup butter, cut into small pieces
2 cups grated sharp Cheddar cheese
3 eggs, beaten
¼ teaspoon Tabasco sauce
salt to taste
black pepper to taste

In a heavy saucepan bring the salt and water to a boil. Slowly stir in the grits. Stir constantly to form a smooth mixture. Lower the heat and cover. Cook for 25 to 35 minutes, stirring occasionally.

Preheat the oven to 350°.

Remove the saucepan from the heat and stir in the butter and cheese. Let the mixture cool to lukewarm.

When the grits are cooled stir in the eggs, Tabasco, salt and pepper.

Heavily butter a 1½-quart casserole. Turn the grits into the casserole and bake for 30 to 40 minutes or until the top is golden brown. Serve hot.

serves 4 to 6

✲ Hominy Grits

5 cups water
1 teaspoon salt
1 cup regular white hominy grits
1 tablespoon butter
salt to taste
black pepper to taste

In a heavy saucepan bring the water and salt to a boil. Slowly stir in the grits. Stir constantly to form a smooth mixture. Lower the heat and cover the saucepan. Cook for 25 to 35 minutes, stirring occasionally. Stir in the butter and season with salt and pepper to taste.

Hominy grits are hominy ground into a coarse meal. Grits are often served as a side dish with butter or gravy or as a breakfast cereal with butter and cream.

serves 4 to 6

❧ Hominy

2 cups whole hominy
2 teaspoons salt
½ cup light cream
½ cup butter

Place the whole hominy in a large bowl. Cover it with warm water and soak overnight.

Drain the soaked hominy and place it in a large pot. Add 3 cups of water and the salt. Simmer for 6 hours or until the hominy is barely tender. Add more water if necessary.

Add the cream and butter and simmer for 1½ to 2 hours longer, or until the hominy is tender. Stir occasionally.

serves 4

❧ Mustard Greens with New Potatoes

2 pounds fresh mustard greens
2 ounces thinly sliced salt pork
12 small new potatoes, quartered
1½ teaspoons salt
½ teaspoon sugar
¼ teaspoon black pepper

Wash the mustard greens thoroughly. Cut off and discard any tough stems and discolored leaves. Cut the greens into pieces 2 to 3 inches long.

Place the salt pork in a large skillet filled with water to a depth of 1 inch. Cover and simmer for 40 to 50 minutes or until the pork is tender.

Add the potatoes to the pork and cook for 5 to 7 minutes. Add more water if necessary. Add the mustard greens, salt and sugar. Cover and cook over medium heat for 15 minutes or until the mustard greens are tender. Do not overcook. Season with pepper and toss well. Serve hot.

serves 6

❧ Smothered Parsnips

6 to 8 small parsnips, peeled
2 tablespoons butter
salt to taste
black pepper to taste
chopped parsley for garnish

Cook the parsnips in a large pot of boiling water until they are tender, about 30 minutes. Drain the parsnips well. When the parsnips are cool enough to handle, cut them lengthwise into strips approximately ½-inch thick.

Melt the butter in a large skillet. Add the parsnips and sprinkle them with salt and pepper. Cover the skillet and cook until the parsnips are lightly browned on both sides, about 8 minutes. Stir often. Serve hot, garnished with the chopped parsley.

serves 4 to 6

❧ Fried Okra

1½ pounds fresh okra
½ teaspoon salt
¼ teaspoon black pepper
½ cup yellow corn meal
1 tablespoon flour
3 tablespoons bacon drippings or lard

Wash and trim the okra. Cut them into ½-inch slices and sprinkle with salt and pepper.

In a shallow bowl, combine the corn meal and flour. Roll the okra slices in the mixture until well coated. Shake off excess.

Heat the bacon drippings in a skillet. When hot, add the coated okra slices and fry until golden brown, about 2 to 5 minutes. Drain on paper towels and serve hot.

serves 6

❧ Creole-Style Stewed Okra

1 tablespoon butter
3 tomatoes, finely chopped, with their juice
1 onion, minced
1 green pepper, minced
1 garlic clove, chopped
salt to taste
black pepper to taste
cayenne pepper to taste
1 teaspoon chopped parsley
3 to 4 dozen fresh okra

In a saucepan melt the butter and add the onion, garlic, and green pepper. Stir well and sauté for 5 to 8 minutes. Add the tomatoes and their juice. Season to taste with the salt, pepper and cayenne pepper. Add the parsley and stir well. Add the okra and simmer for 20 minutes, or until the okra is tender. Serve hot.

serves 6 to 8

❧ Dirty Rice

1½ cups brown rice
3½ cups water
1½ teaspoons salt
2 onions, finely chopped
2 green peppers, finely chopped
4 celery stalks, with leaves, finely chopped
1 garlic clove, finely chopped
2 tablespoons bacon drippings
½ pound chicken giblets, chopped
Tabasco sauce to taste
Worcestershire sauce to taste
salt to taste
black pepper taste
cayenne pepper to taste

Bring the water and salt to a boil in a medium saucepan. Add the rice, cover tightly, and lower the heat. Cook for 50 minutes or until all the water is absorbed. Set the rice aside.

Heat the bacon drippings in a skillet. Add the onions, peppers, celery and garlic. Sauté, stirring often, 30 minutes or until most of the liquid is gone.

Add the chopped chicken giblets (gizzards, livers, and hearts) and sauté until they are browned. Add the Tabasco sauce, Worcestershire sauce, salt, cayenne pepper and pepper to taste. Mix in the rice. Combine well and heat thoroughly. Serve hot.

serves 6 to 8

❧ Southern Rice

1 cup raw long-grain rice
1½ cups cold water
2 tablespoons butter
1 teaspoon lemon juice
1 teaspoon salt

Place the rice in a colander and rinse under cold running water for 2 to 3 minutes. Stir often while rinsing.

Place 1½ cups water in a saucepan. Add the butter, lemon juice and salt. Bring to a boil over high heat. Stir in the rice, cover the saucepan and reduce the heat. Cook until the rice is tender and all the water is absorbed, about 20 minutes.

Remove from the heat and let stand, covered, for 5 to 10 minutes. Fluff with a fork and serve.

serves 4

❧ Carolina Rice Pilau

1 cup raw long-grain rice
1 cup water
1 cup chicken broth
¼ cup shelled pistachio nuts
½ cup pine nuts or toasted slivered almonds
3 tablespoons butter
1 teaspoon powdered mace
½ teaspoon salt

Place the chicken broth and water in a saucepan. Bring to a boil and add the rice. Stir and cover the saucepan. Reduce the heat and simmer until the rice is tender and all the liquid is absorbed, about 20 minutes.

While the rice cooks, melt the butter in a heavy skillet. Add the pistachios and pine nuts and cook for 5 minutes, stirring frequently. The nuts will become golden in color.

Add the rice to the skillet. Season with the mace and salt. Stir until well blended and heated through. Serve immediately.

serves 4 to 6

❧ Red Rice

6 slices bacon
1 cup finely chopped onions
½ cup finely chopped sweet red pepper
1 cup raw long-grain rice
⅛ teaspoon Tabasco sauce
1 teaspoon paprika
1 teaspoon sugar
1 teaspoon salt
2 medium-sized tomatoes, peeled, seeded and
    coarsely chopped
1½ cups cold water

Fry the bacon in a heavy skillet until it is brown and crisp. Drain on paper towels. Crumble and set aside.

Discard all but 4 tablespoons of the bacon fat. Add the onions and red pepper. Sauté, stirring frequently, until the onions are soft but not brown, about 5 minutes. Add the rice and stir until the grains are well coated. Stir in the Tabasco, paprika, sugar, salt, tomatoes and water.

Bring the mixture to a boil over high heat. Cover the skillet, reduce the heat, and simmer for 20 minutes or until the rice is tender. Remove the skillet from the heat and let it stand, covered, for 5 to 10 minutes. Place the rice in a serving bowl, sprinkle with the crumbled bacon and serve.

serves 4

🌿 Wild Rice and Mushrooms

½ pound sliced fresh mushrooms
2 tablespoons finely chopped onions
¼ cup butter
1 cup wild rice, cooked, well-drained, and hot
⅓ cup melted butter

Melt the butter in a skillet. Add the mushrooms and onions and sauté until lightly browned, about 8 minutes.

Cook the wild rice according to the package directions. Do not overcook. Place the cooked and drained wild rice into a serving bowl. Add the mushrooms and onions. Add the melted butter. Mix gently but thoroughly. Serve at once.

serves 4

🌿 Carolina Rice Pilau

1 cup raw long-grain rice
1 cup water
1 cup chicken broth
¼ cup shelled pistachio nuts
½ cup pine nuts or toasted slivered almonds
3 tablespoons butter
1 teaspoon powdered mace
½ teaspoon salt

Place the chicken broth and water in a saucepan. Bring to a boil and add the rice. Stir and cover the saucepan. Reduce the heat and simmer until the rice is done and all the liquid is absorbed, about 20 minutes. While the rice cooks, melt the butter in a heavy skillet. Add the pistachio and pine nuts and cook for several minutes, stirring frequently. The nuts will become golden in color.

Add the rice to the skillet. Season with the mace and salt. Stir until well blended and heated through. Serve immediately.

serves 4 to 6

🌿 Rice Fritters

2 eggs, separated
1 cup sugar
1 cup cooked rice
2 cups flour
2 teaspoons baking powder
oil for frying
confectioner's sugar (optional)

In a large bowl mix together the egg yolks, sugar, rice, flour and baking powder. In a separate bowl, beat the egg whites until stiff but not dry. Fold them into the rice mixture.

In a large deep skillet heat the oil until it is very hot, 370° on a deep-fat thermometer. Drop the rice mixture by tablespoons into the oil and fry until golden, about 3 to 4 minutes.

Remove the rice balls from the oil and drain on paper towels. Dust with confectioner's sugar and serve hot.

serves 4

🌿 Stuffed Acorn Squash

2 acorn squash
1¼ cups chopped apple
½ cup pork sausage meat
3 tablespoons brown sugar
¼ teaspoon nutmeg
¼ teaspoon salt
hot water
4 teaspoons butter

Preheat the oven to 350°.

Halve the squash and scoop out the seeds. Brown the sausage meat in a skillet and drain off the fat.

In a mixing bowl combine the apple, sausage, nutmeg and salt. Stir well. Fill the squash halves with the mixture.

Place the squash in a baking dish. Add just enough hot water to fill the pan to the depth of ½ inch.

Dot each squash half with 1 teaspoon butter and cover the dish tightly with a piece of aluminum foil. Bake for 25 minutes. Remove the foil and bake for 30 minutes longer or until the squash is done.

serves 4

Squash and Corn Pudding

1 pound summer squash, thinly sliced
1 onion, thinly sliced
1 egg
½ cup corn
½ cup heavy cream
½ teaspoon baking powder
½ cup unflavored breadcrumbs
½ cup grated Cheddar cheese
salt to taste
black pepper to taste
butter

Cook the squash and onion over very high heat in a covered pot filled to a depth of 2 inches with water. When the squash and onion are very soft, drain them well and put them into a mixing bowl and mash them together.

Stir in the corn, cream, baking powder, breadcrumbs, grated cheese, salt and pepper. Mix well to blend all the ingredients evenly together.

Preheat the oven to 350°.

Pour the squash and corn mixture into a greased casserole dish. Dot the top of the pudding all over with butter and bake for 1 hour, or until the pudding is golden brown.

serves 6

Turnip Greens and Ham Hock

1 1¾-pound ham hock
2 quarts water
2 bunches turnip greens with turnips
1 teaspoon salt
1 tablespoon sugar
black pepper to taste

Wash the ham hock and place it in a large heavy pot. Add the water and bring to a boil. Lower the heat and simmer gently for 35 to 45 minutes or until the ham hock is tender.

Wash and trim the turnip greens. Discard any discolored leaves. Peel the turnips and cut them in half.

Add the turnip greens, turnips, salt and sugar to the pot with the ham hock. Bring to a boil. Lower the heat and simmer 35 to 45 minutes or until the greens and turnips are tender.

Remove from the heat. Season to taste with black pepper. Spoon the greens and turnips into a serving bowl and serve hot.

serves 6 to 8

Glazed Turnips

1½ pounds turnips, peeled and quartered
4 tablespoons butter
1½ teaspoons sugar
¼ teaspoon grated nutmeg

Melt the butter in a large heavy skillet. Add the turnips and cook over moderate heat for 3 minutes. Stir constantly. Sprinkle the sugar and nutmeg over the turnips and mix well.

Cover the skillet and cook over low heat for 10 minutes, or until the turnips are tender. Serve hot.

serves 6

✺ Fried Tomatoes

4 firm, ripe tomatoes
corn meal
salt to taste
black pepper to taste
bacon drippings
sugar

Remove the stem ends of the tomatoes and cut the tomatoes into ½-inch slices.

Pour some corn meal onto a place and season it with salt and pepper. Combine well. Coat the tomato slices with the corn meal mixture.

In a skillet heat the bacon drippings. When hot, add the coated tomato slices. Fry the tomatoes slowly, turning once, until browned, about 4 to 5 minutes per side. Sprinkle each slice with ½ teaspoon sugar before removing from skillet. Serve at once.

serves 4

✺ Raw Fried Potatoes

6 large potatoes
⅓ cup lard
salt

Peel the potatoes and cut them into thin slices. Place the potato slices in a bowl and add enough water to cover. Soak for 30 minutes or until firm.

Drain the slices and dry them on paper towels.

In a large skillet, heat the lard until it is very hot. Add the potatoes and lower the heat. Fry the potatoes slowly until they are very brown, about 10 to 12 minutes. Turn frequently.

When potatoes are done, remove them from the skillet and drain briefly on paper towels. Salt and serve.

serves 6

✺ Country Fried Potatoes

6 slices bacon
6 potatoes, cooked and chilled
¼ cup bacon drippings
¾ teaspoon salt
⅛ teaspoon black pepper

Fry the bacon in a skillet until brown and crisp. Remove and drain on paper towels. Drain off all but ¼ cup of the bacon drippings.

Peel and slice the chilled potatoes.

Heat the reserved drippings in the skillet. Add the potato slices and season with the salt and pepper. Fry the potatoes over medium heat, turning frequently, until the potatoes are nicely browned, about 10 minutes.

Crumble the bacon slices into the potatoes. Mix well. Remove from heat and serve.

serves 6

✺ Brandied Sweet Potatoes

4 cups hot mashed sweet potatoes
4 tablespoons softened butter
1 tablespoon melted butter
¼ cup sugar
¼ teaspoon ground ginger
¼ teaspoon grated nutmeg
½ teaspoon salt
¼ cup brandy
2 tablespoons light cream

Preheat the oven to 375°.

In a large bowl combine the sweet potatoes, softened butter, sugar, nutmeg, ginger and salt. Mix well. Stir in the brandy and the cream. Combine thoroughly.

Butter a 1-quart casserole dish. Turn the sweet potato mixture into the casserole and brush the top with the melted butter.

Hoppin' John

Southern Fried Chicken

Lime Relish

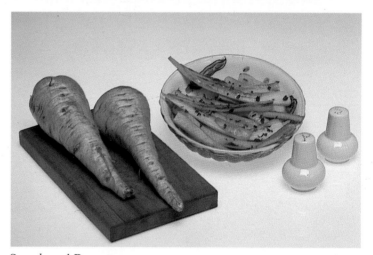

Smothered Parsnips

Collard Greens

Shrimp Bisque

Pecan Corn Muffins

Corn Bread

❧ Breads ❧

To tell the truth, I just can't stand cold weather. I don't ever remember feeling that a north wind was delightfully brisk...it's just downright painful. So what I do on those days when stepping outside is like volunteering for torture is stay *inside* and bake a few loaves of my favorite bread.

Baking bread sends warmth and good feelings through a house like nothing else on this earth. Nobody, but nobody scowls at the aroma of fresh bread, biscuits, or muffins baking in the oven. It is without a doubt one of the nicest things to come home to on a cold winter day.

Here are some of my favorite Southern bread, biscuit and muffin recipes. Everything from traditional Corn Bread, Spoon Bread, and Crackling Bread, to some really interesting and unique recipes for Saffron Bread, Benne Biscuits, Sweet Potato Biscuits, Hoecakes, and Cornsticks. They are all very easy to prepare and bake to perfection every time, even if you've never baked a single thing before.

For those cold winter days, try doubling or tripling some of the recipes and make enough breads, biscuits, or muffins to last an entire week, or surprise some of your friends with a basket of home-baked treats. I think you'll find the reception you get from them will be as warm as the kitchen was.

❧ Benne Biscuits

2 cups flour
1 teaspoon salt
⅛ teaspoon cayenne pepper
¾ cup butter
¼ cup ice water
1 cup sesame seeds
salt

Preheat the oven to 350°.

In a large bowl mix the flour, 1 teaspoon salt and cayenne pepper. With a pastry blender or two knives, cut in the butter. Add enough ice water to make a dough with the consistency of pie crust.

Spread the sesame seeds in a shallow baking dish. Roast them in the oven for 20 minutes, or until the seeds are well browned. Shake the pan during roasting to turn the seeds. Remove the sesame seeds and lower the oven temperature to 300°.

Add the sesame seeds to the dough mixture and stir well. On a lightly floured surface, roll the dough out to ¼-inch thickness. Cut circles from the dough with a small round biscuit cutter. Place the rounds in muffin pans and bake them for 20 to 30 minutes, or until browned. Before removing the biscuits from the pans, sprinkle them with salt. Cool completely.

Store the benne biscuits in tins. To crisp, heat them in a 300° oven before serving.

Benne, or sesame seeds, came to America with slaves from Africa. Dishes made with benne are particularly associated with South Carolina and Charleston.

serves 6

🌿 Bottom-Forty Black Bread

2 cups warm water
1 package active dried yeast
2 tablespoons brown sugar
2 teaspoons salt
2 tablespoons corn oil
4 cups sifted white flour
3 tablespoons dark molasses
3 cups rye flour
1 tablespoon dill seeds
1 tablespoon poppy seeds

In a large bowl dissolve the dried yeast in the warm water. Add the brown sugar, salt, oil and flour to the bowl and mix well. Add the molasses, rye flour, dill seeds and poppy seeds and mix into a stiff dough (use more white flour if necessary).

Knead the dough on a floured board until it is very elastic and extremely smooth. Grease a large bowl (at least twice the size of the dough). Put the dough in the bowl and turn to coat it. Cover the bowl with a towel let the dough rise in a warm, draft-free place until doubled in size.

Divide the dough in half and shape each half into a ball. Place the two dough balls on a greased baking sheet and punch the dough down, flattening it a little. Place the baking sheet in a warm place, cover it with a cheesecloth or light towel and let rise until it is doubled in size.

Preheat the oven at 400°.

Bake the breads for 30 minutes. Brush the loaves with water (or egg white for a crisp, shiny crust) every 10 minutes. The loaves are done when they sound hollow when tapped.

makes 2 loaves

🌿 Breakfast Bread

1 cup warm water
1 package active dried yeast
½ cup honey
1 teaspoon salt
2½ cups flour
1 egg
½ cup corn oil
2 teaspoons grated lemon rind
½ cup chopped walnuts
½ cup white currants
½ cup raspberry preserves or drained canned
   raspberries

Put the warm water in a mixing bowl and dissolve the yeast in it. Stir in the honey, salt and 1½ cups of the flour. Beat with electric mixer until smooth, about 2 minutes. Beat in the egg, corn oil, lemon rind, walnuts and currants. Mix thoroughly until well blended.

Turn the dough out onto a lightly floured surface. With your hands, pound the dough into a flat oblong about 8 inches wide. Spread the raspberry preserves or canned raspberries on top of the flattened dough. Roll up the dough into a loaf shape and place it in a buttered 1½-quart baking dish. Cover the loaf with a towel and let it rise in a warm place until it is doubled in size.

Preheat the oven to 375°.

Bake the bread for 30 minutes, brushing with beaten egg white every 10 minutes for a shiny, crisp crust.

makes 1 loaf

🥨 Buttermilk Biscuits

2 cups flour
1 teaspoon baking powder
½ teaspoon baking soda
1 teaspoon salt
4 tablespoons softened butter
1 cup thick buttermilk

Sift the flour, baking powder, baking soda and salt into a mixing bowl. Cut in the butter with a pastry blender or two knives until the mixture resembles a coarse meal. Add enough of the buttermilk to make a soft dough. Mix lightly.

Turn the dough out onto a lightly floured surface. Knead for about 5 minutes.

Preheat the oven to 450°.

Roll out the dough on a floured surface to ½-inch thickness. Cut the dough into rounds with a 2-inch floured biscuit cutter.

Place the biscuits on lightly greased baking sheets. Bake for 10 to 12 minutes. Serve hot.

makes 12 to 14 biscuits

🥨 Drop Biscuits

2 cups flour
2 teaspoons baking powder
1 teaspoon salt
4 tablespoons butter
1 cup milk

Preheat the oven to 450°.

Combine the flour with the baking powder and salt in a large bowl. Cut in the butter with a pastry blender or two knives until the mixture resembles a coarse meal. Add the milk and stir to form a soft dough.

Drop the dough by well-rounded tablespoons onto a lightly buttered cookie sheet. There should be 12 biscuits.

Bake for 12 to 15 minutes or until golden. Serve hot.

makes 1 dozen

🥨 Cheese Biscuits

¼ pound butter
1 cup flour
¾ cup grated Swiss cheese
½ tablespoon French-style mustard
2 egg yolks, beaten
⅛ teaspoon cayenne pepper

Preheat the oven to 300°.

In a bowl beat the butter until very creamy. Add the egg yolks and mix well. Add the grated cheese, mustard and cayenne pepper. Gradually stir in the flour. Mix thoroughly to make a stiff dough.

Roll out the dough on a lightly floured surface. Cut small biscuits with a floured 1-inch biscuit cutter.

Place the biscuits on a greased baking sheet and bake for 20 minutes or until golden. Serve hot.

serves 6 to 8

❧ Cornsticks

1½ cups corn meal
½ cup flour
1 teaspoon baking soda
1 teaspoon baking powder
2 tablespoons sugar
2 eggs, beaten
2 cups buttermilk
3 tablespoons melted butter

Preheat the oven to 425°.

In a large bowl combine the flour, baking soda, salt, baking powder and sugar. Stir in the corn meal.

In another bowl combine the eggs, buttermilk and melted butter. Add to the flour mixture and beat well.

Butter the molds of a 12-stick cast-iron cornstick pan. Spoon the batter into the molds, filling them two-thirds full.

Bake for 20 to 25 minutes or until golden brown. Serve at once.

makes 12 cornsticks

❧ Corn Bread

2 tablespoons bacon fat or butter
1½ cups corn meal
1½ teaspoons baking powder
3 tablespoons flour
½ teaspoon salt
1½ cups milk
1 egg

Preheat the oven to 450°.

Melt the bacon fat or butter in a heavy 12-inch iron skillet.

In a mixing bowl combine the corn meal, flour, salt and baking powder. Add the milk and egg. Mix well.

Add the melted butter and stir to blend. Pour the batter into the hot iron skillet.

Place the skillet in the oven and bake 20 to 25 minutes or until golden brown. Serve warm with butter.

Although this bread can be made in a baking dish, for true authenticity it must be made in a cast-iron skillet.

makes 1 corn bread

❧ Old-Fashioned Crackling Bread

2 cups cracklings
3 cups corn meal
1 teaspoon salt
1 teaspoon baking soda
¼ cup corn oil
buttermilk

Soak the cracklings in a bowl with enough hot water to cover until tender. Drain.

Preheat the oven to 350°.

Combine all the ingredients in a mixing bowl and add enough buttermilk to make a stiff but workable batter. Press the batter into a greased square cake or biscuit pan. Bake for 30 minutes. Cut and serve warm.

serves 12

Down-Home Raisin Bread

1 pound black raisins
ground cinnamon
½ cup honey
warm water
5 cups flour
1 cup butter
2 cups sugar
4 eggs
1½ teaspoons grated nutmeg
1 package active dried yeast
2 cups hot milk

Put the raisins into a mixing bowl and sprinkle with enough cinnamon to cover the surface.

Thin the honey with just enough warm water so that it pours easily. Add the honey to the mixing bowl. Mix well and set aside.

Cream the butter and sugar together in a mixing bowl until smooth. Add the eggs, one at a time, beating continuously.

Mix the nutmeg, yeast and flour together in another bowl. Blend the flour into the butter-sugar mixture alternately with the heated milk. If the dough becomes too soft to be workable, add more flour.

Turn the dough out onto a lightly floured surface. With your hands, pound the dough into an oblong 9 inches wide and as flat as you can make it. Cover the surface of the dough with the honey and raisin mixture, then roll the dough up like a jelly roll.

Place the roll in a greased bowl, turning it to grease all sides. Cover the bowl with a towel and let it rise in a warm place until it is doubled in size.

Punch dough down and divide it in half. Put each loaf into a buttered loaf pan. Cover the pans with towels and let the dough rise again until it is doubled in size.

Preheat the oven to 325°.

Bake the loaves for 1½ hours, or until the loaves are brown and sound hollow when tapped. Turn the loaves out of the pans and cool on racks.

makes 2 loaves

Hush Puppies

1½ cups white corn meal
½ cup flour
⅛ teaspoon salt
2 tablespoons baking powder
½ teaspoon baking soda
1 egg
1 cup buttermilk
1 onion, finely chopped
4 tablespoons melted bacon drippings, lard or vegetable oil

In a large bowl combine the flour, salt, baking powder and baking soda. Mix well. Stir in the corn meal. Add the egg and beat the mixture with a wooden spoon until it is smooth.

Pour in the buttermilk and stir until it is absorbed by the corn meal mixture. Stir in the onion.

In a deep skillet, heat the bacon drippings until very hot, 375° on a deep-frying thermometer. The fat should be to a depth of 2 to 3 inches in the skillet.

Drop the hush puppies by rounded teaspoons into the fat. Fry, turning frequently, until golden, about 3 minutes. Serve warm with butter.

makes 12 hush puppies

❧ Hoecakes

1 cup white corn meal
½ teaspon salt
¾ cup boiling water
1 to 2 tablespoons bacon fat or butter

In a mixing bowl combine the corn meal and the salt. In a slow, continuous stream, pour in the boiling water; stir constantly. Beat until the batter is smooth.

To form the hoecakes, scoop up approximately 2 tablespoons of the batter and gently pat it into a flat circle about 3½ to 4 inches in diameter.

Heat 1 tablespoon bacon fat in a heavy skillet. When the fat is very hot, reduce the heat and add 4 hoecakes. Fry for about 2 minutes per side or until golden brown. Turn carefully.

Remove the fried hoecakes. Add the remaining 4 hoecakes and fry. Add the remaining fat if needed. Serve hot.

makes 8 hoecakes

❧ Pecan Corn Muffins

3½ cups whole wheat flour
1 cup yellow corn meal
1 package active dry yeast
1 teaspoon baking powder
1 teaspoon salt
1 cup milk
8 tablespoons butter
½ cup water
⅓ cup honey
2 eggs
1 cup coarsely chopped pecans

Grease 18 muffin-tin cups. Sprinkle each cup with a little bit of corn meal. Set aside.

In a large bowl, combine 1 cup of the whole wheat flour, the corn meal, yeast, baking powder and salt.

Place the milk, butter, water and honey in a saucepan. Heat the mixture until the butter melts. Set aside and cool until lukewarm.

When the milk mixture has cooled, pour it into the flour mixture. With an electric mixer, beat the batter at medium speed for 2 minutes. Beat in the eggs. Remove from mixer and stir in the remaining flour. Add the pecans and stir. The dough should be a little lumpy.

Fill each muffin cup three-quarters full with the dough. Smooth the tops. Cover the muffin tins with clean towels and let the dough rise in a warm place for 40 to 50 minutes or until the dough almost fills the tins.

Preheat the oven to 350°.

Bake the muffins for 20 minutes or until golden brown. Serve warm.

makes 18 muffins

Saffron Bread

¼ teaspoon crumbled saffron threads
½ cup boiling water
2 cups milk
¼ pound melted butter
1 package active dry yeast
2 tablespoons warm water
1 cup sugar
½ teaspoon salt
½ teaspoon nutmeg
6 to 6½ cups sifted flour
grated rinds of 2 lemons
2 cups currants
1 tablespoon melted butter

In a small bowl, steep the saffron in the boil ing water for 1 hour. Strain and reserve the saffron liquid.

In a saucepan, scald the milk and place it in a large mixing bowl. Add the saffron liquid and the melted butter. Stir well.

Dissolve the yeast in the warm water. Stir it into the warm milk mixture. Add the sugar, salt and nutmeg. Sift in the flour and mix well. Add the grated lemon rind and the currants. Mix the dough until well blended. The dough should be stiff.

Cover the mixing bowl with a clean towel. Let the dough rise in a warm place until it is doubled in bulk, about 1½ hours.

Remove the dough from the bowl. Punch it down and knead it on a lightly floured surface until smooth, about 2 minutes.

Butter two 9 × 5 × 3-inch loaf pans.

Divide the dough and shape each half into a loaf. Place the halves in the loaf pans. Let the dough rise a second time, about 50 to 60 minutes.

Preheat the oven to 350°.

Bake the loaves for 1 hour or until they are golden and sound hollow when tapped.

Remove the pans to cooling racks and brush the tops of the loaves with melted butter. Cool in the pans for 10 minutes. Turn the loaves out onto racks and continue cooling. Cool completely before slicing.

makes 2 loaves

Spoon Bread

1 cup white corn meal
½ teaspoon salt
1½ cups boiling water
2 eggs, separated
1 tablespoon melted butter
1 cup buttermilk
½ teaspoon baking soda

Preheat the oven to 325°.

In a large bowl mix the corn meal and salt. Add the boiling water and egg yolks. Mix well. Add the butter and buttermilk. Stir until well blended.

In a separate bowl beat the egg whites and the baking soda until stiff but not dry. Fold the egg whites into the batter.

Grease a 1½- or 2-quart baking dish. Pour the batter into the dish. Bake for 45 minutes. Remove from the oven and serve immediately.

serves 4 to 6

🌿 Sweet Potato Biscuits

1 cup flour
1 teaspoon baking powder
½ tablespoon salt
1 small sweet potato, cooked, peeled and diced
2 tablespoons butter
1 to 3 tablespoons milk

Preheat the oven to 400°.

Sift the flour, baking powder and salt together into a large bowl. Cut the sweet potato pieces and butter into the mixture, using a pastry blender or two knives. Add the milk and stir until well blended.

Turn the dough out onto a lightly floured surface and knead for 2 minutes. Roll the dough out to ½-inch thickness. Cut the dough into rounds with a floured 2-inch biscuit cutter.

Place the biscuits on a greased baking sheet and bake for 12 minutes or until golden. Serve hot.

makes 10 to 12 biscuits

🌿 Sweet Potato Rolls

1 large sweet potato
1 package active dry yeast
¾ teaspoon salt
3 tablespoons sugar
1 tablespoon butter
1 cup milk
3½ to 4½ cups flour

Peel the sweet potato and cut it into thirds. Place the pieces in a saucepan and add enough cold water to cover. Cook the sweet potato until tender, about 15 to 20 minutes. Drain and reserve ¼ cup of the cooking water.

When the cooking water has cooled to lukewarm, add the yeast to it and stir to dissolve.

Place the sweet potato pieces into a large mixing bowl. Mash the pieces with a fork and then add the salt, sugar and butter. Beat well.

Place the milk in a saucepan and heat until a skin begins to form on top. Skim the milk and stir it into the sweet potato mixture. Allow the mixture to cool to lukewarm. When cooled, stir in the yeast and water mixture.

Add to the sweet potato mixture as much flour as necessary, 1 cup at a time, to make dough dense enough to knead. Turn the dough out onto a floured surface and knead until it is smooth and elastic. Place the dough in a large, oiled bowl and cover it with a clean towel. Let the dough rise in a warm place until it is doubled in size, about 1½ hours.

Remove the dough from the bowl and punch it down.

Grease the cups of two 10-cup muffin tins. Pinch off 20 small pieces of the dough and place one in each cup. Set the tins aside and let the dough rise again until it is almost doubled or until the cups are almost filled, about 45 to 50 minutes.

Preheat the oven to 425°.

Bake the muffins for 13 to 15 minutes or until golden. Allow them to cool slightly before serving.

makes 20 rolls

❧ Creole Honey Bread

2 cups flour
1 teaspoon baking soda
1 teaspoon baking powder
1 teaspoon salt
1 teaspoon ground ginger
½ teaspoon cinnamon
1 cup milk
1 cup honey
1 egg, slightly beaten

Preheat the oven to 375°.

Into a large bowl sift the flour, baking soda, baking powder, salt, ginger and cinnamon. Stir in the milk, honey and egg. Place in the bowl of an electric mixer and beat for 20 minutes or until all ingredients are well blended and the batter is smooth.

Pour the batter into a buttered 9 × 5 × 3-inch loaf pan. Bake for 45 minutes or until a cake tester inserted in the middle comes out clean.

Remove the bread from the oven and cool in the pan for 10 minutes. Turn the loaf out onto a rack and continue cooling. Serve the bread sliced thin.

makes 1 loaf

❧ Pecan Bread

3½ cups flour
1 cup sugar
1 teaspoon salt
3 teaspoons baking powder
1 cup milk
2 cups chopped pecans
¼ cup melted butter or lard
1 egg

Preheat the oven to 350°

In a large bowl combine the flour, sugar, salt and baking powder. Mix well. Add the milk, egg and melted butter. Stir until well blended and the batter is smooth. Stir in the pecans.

Butter a 9 × 5 × 3-inch pan. Pour the batter into the pan and bake for 1 hour, or until a cake tester inserted into the middle comes out clean.

Remove from oven. Cool in the pan for 10 minutes, then turn the loaf out onto a rack and cool completely.

makes 1 loaf

❧ Peach and Walnut Bread

¼ cup butter
½ cup sugar
1 egg
2½ cups flour
3 teaspoons baking powder
1 teaspoon salt
1 cup milk
¾ cup chopped walnuts
1 cup chopped dried peaches

Preheat the oven to 375°.

Combine the flour with the baking powder and salt in a large bowl or on a large sheet of waxed paper.

In a mixing bowl cream together the butter, sugar and egg. Add the flour mixture to the creamed mixture alternately with the milk. Stir in the walnuts and peaches.

Turn the batter into a buttered 9 × 5 × 3-inch loaf pan. Bake for 50 to 55 minutes or until a cake tester inserted in the center of the loaf comes out clean.

Remove from the oven to a cooling rack. Cool in the pan for 10 minutes, then turn out onto the rack and cool completely.

makes 1 loaf

🦋 Rice Bread

1 cup cooked cold rice, pushed through a sieve
2 cups white corn meal
3 eggs
1 tablespoon melted butter
2½ teaspoons baking powder
2¼ cups milk
1 teaspoon salt

Preheat the oven to 400°.

In a bowl beat the eggs lightly. Gradually pour in the milk and mix well.

In another bowl combine the corn meal, salt and baking powder. Add to the egg mixture and beat well. Add the melted butter and sieved rice. Beat until the batter is very light.

Butter a shallow 9 × 9-inch baking pan and fill with the batter. Bake for 30 minutes or until golden. Serve hot with butter.

makes 1 loaf

🦋 Corn Meal Mush

3 cups corn meal
3 cups cold water
12 cups boiling water
salt to taste
oil or butter for frying

Mix the corn meal with the water in a very large pot. Heat the mixture and then add the *boiling* water. Stir constantly to break up lumps. Add salt to taste.

Boil the mixture for 35 minutes over moderate heat. When done, pour into 2 or 3 greased loaf pans. Place the pans in the refrigerator. When the corn meal mush is chilled, cut it into thin slices. Fry the slices and serve them with bacon.

makes 2 to 3 molded loaves

🦋 Huckleberry Bread

2 eggs
1 cup sugar
3 tablespoons melted butter
1 cup milk
3 cups flour
1 teaspoon salt
4 teaspoons baking powder
1 cup fresh huckleberries
½ cup chopped walnuts

Preheat the oven to 350°.

In a large bowl beat the eggs. Gradually add the sugar and continue beating for 1 minute. Add the butter and milk. Stir until well blended.

In a bowl combine the huckleberries and the chopped nuts.

Combine the flour with salt and baking powder. Add to the huckleberries and nuts and stir gently. Add the mixture to the egg and milk mixture. Stir only until the dry ingredients are moistened.

Turn the dough into a buttered 5 × 12-inch loaf pan. Bake for 50 to 60 minutes or until a cake tester inserted into the center comes out clean.

Remove to a cooling rack and cool in the pan for 10 minutes. Turn out onto the rack and cool completely.

makes 1 loaf

🦋 Corn Muffins

2 cups yellow corn meal
1 teaspoon salt
2 cups boiling water
1 cup cold milk
2 eggs, beaten
4 teaspoons baking powder
2 tablespoons melted butter

Preheat the oven to 375°

Combine the corn meal and salt in a mixing bowl.

Pour the *boiling* water over the corn meal. Stir immediately. It is crucial that the water be boiling when it is poured.

Add the milk immediately. Add the eggs and stir well. Mix in the baking powder and butter. Stir well.

Pour the batter into greased muffin pans. Bake for 20 to 25 minutes or until golden brown.

makes 12 muffins

Southern-Style Popovers

1½ cups flour
¼ teaspoon salt
2 eggs, lightly beaten
1½ cups milk
2 tablespoons melted butter

Preheat the oven to 425°.

In a large bowl sift together the flour and salt. Add the eggs, milk and butter. Blend well to make a smooth batter.

Beat the batter with an electric mixer for 3 minutes.

Lightly butter one 12-cup muffin tin or two 6-cup tins that have been warmed in the oven for 5 minutes. Fill the cups two-thirds full with the batter.

Bake for 30 minutes. Do not open the oven while the popovers bake. They will brown and pop when done. Serve hot.

makes 12 popovers

Blueberry Muffins

2½ cups ripe blueberries
2 cups flour
2 teaspoons baking powder
½ teaspoon salt
½ cup butter
1 cup sugar
2 eggs
½ cup milk

Preheat the oven to 375°.

Rinse the blueberries and remove any stems and blemished berries. Dry the berries completely on paper towels.

Mash ½ cup of the blueberries in small bowl until smooth. Set aside.

Place the remaining berries in a bowl with 2 tablespoons flour. Toss to coat the berries and set aside.

Combine the remaining flour with the baking powder and salt in a bowl or on a large piece of waxed paper.

In a mixing bowl cream the butter and sugar together until light and fluffy. Add the eggs, 1 at a time. Beat well after each addition.

Add 1 cup of the flour mixture to the creamed mixture. Mix well. Beat in half the milk. Beat in the remaining flour and the rest of the milk. Continue to beat until the batter is smooth. Add the mashed berries and beat again. Fold the whole berries into the batter. Mix gently.

Spoon the batter into 20 well-buttered muffin cups, filling each about three-quarters full.

Bake for 20 to 25 minutes or until a cake tester inserted into the center of a muffin comes out clean.

Remove from the oven. Turn the muffins out of the tins and serve warm.

makes 20 muffins

❧ Desserts ❧

I'm sure there's someone among your family and friends—and I don't necessarily mean the kids —who thinks that sweets and treats are the best part of your dinner. I have one particular friend who comes by from time to time, and by the darnedest luck, it's always just as we're ready for dessert and coffee. After years of practice, he's got his timing perfected. As soon as the last dinner plate is cleared off the table, there's the familiar two knocks on the back door, and then, "Just thought I'd drop by to say hi and—oh, you're still eating. Well, I'll just come back a little later on, and…unless, of course, there's enough to go round." Just coincidence…of course.

Well, if you know some people who would go out of their way for something sweet, then be prepared to be loved beyond all rational reason when you make the desserts on the following pages. Once the word gets around about your Kentucky Bourbon Cake or Charlotte Russe, you may find yourself cooking dinner for a family of five and cooking dessert for a crowd of ten!

Desserts like Key Lime Pie are tart and tangy enough to cut the edge off a big meal; or Fruit and Rice Pudding is so sweet, smooth and creamy it melts in your mouth; Jam Cake with Fruit Frosting, Pecan Butter Balls…these desserts are the kind that can make you a neighborhood legend.

❧ Blackberry Cake

1½ cups sugar
½ cup butter
2 eggs
1 cup fresh blackberries
2 cups flour
½ teaspoon baking powder
1 teaspoon grated nutmeg
½ teaspoon cinnamon
⅔ cup buttermilk
1 teaspoon baking soda

Preheat the oven to 350°. Butter and flour a 13 × 9 × 2-inch baking pan. Set aside.

In a mixing bowl combine the sugar, butter, eggs and blackberries. Beat the mixture with an electric mixer at medium-high for 2 minutes.

In a separate bowl combine the flour, baking powder, nutmeg and cinnamon.

Combine the buttermilk and baking soda in a bowl. Add alternately with the flour mixture to the berries. Beat for 2 minutes.

Pour the batter into the pan and bake for 25 to 30 mintues, or until a cake tester inserted into the center of the cake comes out clean.

Remove and let cool. Serve from baking pan.

serves 10 to 12

🦐 Charleston Torte

3 eggs
1½ cups sugar
¼ cup flour
1 teaspoon baking powder
¼ teaspoon salt
1 cup finely chopped apples
1 cup finely chopped pecans
1 teaspoon pure vanilla extract
1 cup chilled heavy cream
2 tablespoons chopped pecans

Preheat the oven to 400°. Generously butter a 12 × 8 × 2-inch baking pan. Set aside.

Sift together the flour, baking powder and salt. Set aside.

Beat the eggs briefly. Then add the sugar and vanilla and beat until the mixture is thick, about 4 to 5 minutes.

Beat in the flour mixture until well blended. Add the chopped apples and the chopped pecans. Mix them gently but thoroughly into the batter with a rubber spatula.

Turn the batter into the pan and bake for 30 to 35 minutes, or until a cake tester inserted into the center comes out clean.

Remove the cake from the oven and cool slightly.

Beat the cream in a chilled mixing bowl until it is stiff. Transfer the cream to a serving bowl and sprinkle it with the 2 tablespoons chopped pecans. Serve the cake directly from the baking pan while it is still warm. Serve the whipped cream on the side.

serves 8 to 10

🦐 Charlotte Russe

2 cups heavy cream
1 teaspoon pure vanilla extract
½ cup sugar
4 teaspoons sweet sherry
½ tablespoon unflavored gelatin
water
½ cup warm milk
5 egg whites
ladyfinger halves

In a large bowl, whip the cream until it forms firm peaks. Stir in the vanilla, sugar and sherry.

Soften the unflavored gelatin in a small bowl with enough water to cover. Add the warm milk and stir. When the gelatin mixture has cooled, beat it into the cream mixture with an electric beater.

In another bowl, beat the egg whites until they are stiff. Fold the egg whites into the cream and gelatin mixture.

Line a glass bowl with halved ladyfingers. Pour the Charlotte Russe mixture over them. Chill in the refrigerator until firm and serve cold.

serves 6

🌿 Colonial Cherry Pudding

½ cup softened butter
1 cup sugar
1 egg
2 teaspoons baking powder
1½ cups flour
⅔ cups milk
1 teaspoon pure vanilla extract
2 cups canned, whole pitted cherries (save the juice)
1 tablespoon blackberry brandy (optional)
1 cup heavy cream

Cream the butter and sugar together in a mixing bowl. Beat in the egg and baking powder. Add the flour and milk alternately, a little at a time, while stirring. Stir in the vanilla, then fold in the cherries and blackberry brandy.

Pour the batter into a buttered loaf pan. Bake for 1 hour, or until the pudding is firm but still moist.

In a large bowl, whip the cream until it forms firm peaks. Add the reserved cherry juice. Top each pudding serving with the cream.

serves 8

🌿 Coconut Jumbles

⅔ cup butter
1 cup sugar
1 egg, beaten
1 cup flour
1 cup freshly grated coconut

Preheat the oven to 375°.

Heavily grease 2 baking sheets and set aside.

Cream the butter in a large mixing bowl. Add the sugar and continue creaming until the mixture is light and fluffy. Add the egg and mix well. Stir in the flour and mix well. Gradually add the coconut and mix until the batter is stiff.

Drop the batter by well-rounded teaspoons onto the baking sheets. Bake for 5 to 7 minutes, or until the cookies are lightly browned.

Cool the cookies for 30 seconds on the baking sheets and then remove to cooling racks. Cool completely.

makes approximately 36 cookies

🌿 Fruit and Rice Pudding

½ cup sugar
1 egg, well beaten
2 cups cooked white rice
2 cups light cream
½ pound dates, chopped
½ pound dried apricots, chopped
½ pound seedless white grapes, chopped
1 cup chopped pecans
grated rind of 1 lemon
½ teaspoon ground ginger
½ teaspoon grated nutmeg
½ teaspoon pure vanilla extract
2 tablespoons melted butter

Preheat the oven to 350°.

In a large mixing bowl, mix the sugar, egg and rice together. Add the cream, dates, apricots, grapes, pecans, lemon rind, ginger, nutmeg and vanilla. Mix well.

Pour the pudding into a buttered baking dish. Bake for 30 minutes, or until the pudding is set and lightly browned on top.

Serve warm or cold with vanilla sauce or sweet cream.

serves 6

🌿 Frosted Fig Cake

2 cups white flour
1 cup brown sugar
1 teaspoon salt
1 teaspoon baking soda
1 teaspoon ground cinnamon
1 teaspoon ground cloves
½ teaspoon ground ginger
1 teaspoon grated nutmeg
1 cup vegetable oil
3 eggs, well beaten
¾ cup buttermilk
1½ cups fig preserves or chopped candied figs
½ cup shelled roasted sunflower seeds
1 cup chopped pecans
1 tablespoon pure vanilla extract
Frosting:
½ cup buttermilk
1 cup sugar
1 tablespoon corn syrup
½ teaspoon baking soda
½ cup vegetable oil
1 teaspoon almond extract

Preheat the oven to 325°.

Combine the flour, brown sugar, salt, baking soda, cinnamon, cloves, ginger and nutmeg in a mixing bowl. Add the vegetable oil and eggs and beat until smooth. Slowly add the buttermilk, fig preserves or candied figs, sunflower seeds, pecans and vanilla. Stir constantly with a wooden spoon or beat with an electric mixer on low until the batter is smooth.

Pour the batter into a greased 10-inch cake pan. Bake for 1 hour, or until cake is moist but not sticky when tested with a toothpick.

While the cake is baking, make the frosting (it's really more like a sauce). Mix the buttermilk, sugar, corn syrup, baking soda and oil in a saucepan over low heat. Slowly raise the heat to medium, making sure the buttermilk does not scorch, and stir the mixture continuously until it reaches a slow boil. Cook for 3 or 4 minutes, stirring constantly. Remove the saucepan from the heat and stir in the almond extract.

Remove the cake from the baking pan and cool on a rack. Pour the frosting over the cake, sprinkle some cinnamon and confectioner's sugar over the top, and serve.

serves 6

🌿 Huckleberry Pie

1 quart fresh huckleberries
3 tablespoons quick-cooking tapioca
1 cup sugar
¼ teaspoon salt
juice of 1 lemon
1 pastry for 2-crust, 9-inch pie
1 tablespoon butter, cut into pieces

Preheat the oven to 450°.

In a large bowl combine the huckleberries, tapioca, sugar, salt and lemon juice. Set aside.

Roll out the pastry on a lightly floured surface. Fit half of it into a 9-inch pie plate. Trim the edges.

Pour the berry mixture into the pie shell. Dot with butter.

Cover the pie with the remaining pastry. Moisten the edges with a little water and flute to seal. Cut several vents in the top.

Bake the pie for 10 minutes. Reduce the heat to 350° and bake for 30 to 35 minutes longer. Serve warm or cold.

Huckleberries have a stronger flavor than blueberries, but are otherwise much the same.

serves 6 to 8

🍃 Jam Cake

¾ cup softened butter
1 cup sugar
3 eggs
3 cups flour
2 teaspoons baking powder
1 teaspoon baking soda
¼ teaspoon salt
1 teaspoon ground cinnamon
½ cup buttermilk
1 cup thick blackberry jam

Preheat the oven to 350°. Grease 2 9-inch round cake pans. Set aside.

In a large mixing bowl cream the butter and sugar until light and fluffy. Add the eggs and beat well.

In a bowl or on a large sheet of wax paper, sift together the flour, baking powder, baking soda and cinnamon 3 times.

Add the flour mixture to the creamed mixture alternately with the buttermilk. End with the flour. Fold in the jam.

Turn the batter into the prepared cake pans. Distribute it evenly. Bake the cakes for 35 to 45 minutes, or until they are golden brown.

Remove the cakes to cooling racks and cool in the pans for 10 minutes. Turn out onto racks and continue cooling.

Frost with Fruit Frosting (see below).

Jam cake is a favorite in Kentucky and Tennessee. Use only berry jam.

makes 1 cake

🍃 Fruit Frosting

½ cup pitted dates
1½ cups raisins
1 orange, peeled
1 lemon, peeled
⅓ cup sugar

Grind the dates and raisins together and place them in a saucepan.

Cut the orange and lemon into pieces and remove all the seeds. Grind the pieces together and add them to the saucepan.

Add the sugar to the saucepan and cook over medium heat until the mixture thickens. Stir constantly. Spread the frosting over the cake while still warm.

To frost the jam cake, place one cake layer top-side down on a serving plate. Brush off any crumbs. Spread with about one-third the frosting mixture. Place the second layer, top-side up, on top. Frost the sides of both layers and then frost the top. Smooth the frosting. Allow the frosting to set for a few hours before cutting the cake.

makes enough for 1 2-layer cake

🍃 Kentucky Bourbon Balls

1 6-ounce package semisweet chocolate pieces
½ cup sugar
2 tablespoons light corn syrup
⅓ cup Bourbon whiskey
7 ounces finely ground vanilla wafers
1 cup finely chopped walnuts
1 cup finely ground pecans or almonds

In the top of a double boiler over hot but not boiling water, melt the chocolate pieces.

Remove the double boiler from the heat and stir in the sugar, corn syrup and Bourbon.

In a mixing bowl combine the wafer crumbs and the walnuts. Stir in the chocolate mixture. Blend well.

Immediately shape the mixture into 1-inch balls and roll them in the ground pecans.

Store in an airtight container for at least 7 days before serving.

makes approximately 50 balls

Pound Cake

Spoon Bread

Pecan Pie

Bottom Forty Black Bread

Beefy Okra Soup

❧ Pecan Butter Balls

½ cup butter
2 tablespoons sugar
1 teaspoon pure vanilla extract
1 cup flour
⅛ teaspoon salt
1 cup finely ground pecans
confectioner's sugar

Preheat the oven to 375°.

In a large bowl cream the butter and sugar together until they are light and fluffy. Add the vanilla and mix well.

Add the flour and salt to the creamed mixture and mix well. Add the nuts and stir until thoroughly combined.

Drop the batter by well-rounded teaspoons onto ungreased baking sheets. Bake for 20 minutes.

Remove the balls from the oven and cool for 1 minute on the baking sheets. Roll each ball in confectioner's sugar and continue cooling. Store in the refrigerator.

yields approximately 36 cookies

❧ Pecan Pralines

1 pound light brown sugar
1 cup pecan halves
4 tablespoons butter
4 tablespoons water

Chop ⅓ cup of the pecans coarsely. Chop another ⅓ cup of the pecans finely. Leave the remaining ⅓ cup in halves.

Place the sugar, butter and water in a saucepan over low heat. Bring to a boil, stirring constantly.

When the syrup begins to boil, add all the pecans and stir. Cook until mixture begins to bubble. Remove the saucepan from the heat.

Pour the mixture out onto a flat surface covered with wax paper or onto a marble slab. Let the candy harden. When hard, break into serving pieces.

❧ Southern Rum Pie

1 pastry for 2-crust, 9-inch pie
1 cup light brown sugar
¾ teaspoon cinnamon
¼ cup flour
⅛ teaspoon salt
6 cups peeled, cored and thinly sliced apples
2 tablespoons butter, cut into small pieces
2 tablespoons dark rum

Preheat the oven to 425°.

Roll out the pastry on a lightly floured surface. Fit half of it into a 9-inch pie plate.

In a small bowl combine the sugar, cinnamon, flour and salt.

Place the sliced apples in a large bowl. Add the sugar mixture and mix lightly. Arrange the apple-sugar mixture in the pie plate and dot with the butter.

Roll out the remaining pastry on a lightly floured surface. Make slits in the center and fit it over the filling. Seal the edges together, trim and flute.

Bake for 45 to 50 minutes, or until the crust is golden. Remove the pie from the oven and put it on a cooling rack. Pour the rum through the slits in the upper crust. Serve warm.

serves 6 to 8

❧ Pound Cake

1 pound butter
1 pound sugar
10 eggs, separated
4 cups flour
½ teaspoon salt
1 teaspoon baking powder
1 teaspoon pure vanilla extract
2 tablespoons grated lemon rind

Butter 2 12-inch loaf pans and dust them lightly with flour. Set aside.

Cream the butter in a large bowl. Gradually add the sugar and continue creaming until the mixture is light and fluffy.

In a separate bowl beat the egg yolks. Add the yolks to the butter mixture, beating constantly.

In a bowl or on a large sheet of wax paper, sift together the flour, salt and baking powder 4 times.

Gradually add the flour to the butter mixture. Mix thoroughly.

Preheat the oven to 300°.

In a small bowl beat the egg whites until they are stiff but not dry. Fold the egg whites into the batter.

Pour half the mixture into each of the loaf pans. Bake for 1 to 1¼ hours, or until a cake tester inserted into the middle of the loaf comes out clean.

Remove the pans to cooling racks. Cool 10 minutes in the pan. Then turn out onto racks and cool completely. Serve sliced with a fruit sauce.

A traditional pound cake such as this one calls for one pound each of the major ingredients. Ten eggs weigh about one pound.

makes 2 loaf cakes

❧ Coconut Pound Cake

1½ cups softened butter
2½ cups sugar
5 eggs, at room temperature
3 cups flour
1 teaspoon baking powder
1 teaspoon almond extract
1 teaspoon pure vanilla extract
1 cup light cream
1 cup grated coconut

Butter and lightly flour a 10-inch tube pan. Set aside.

In a large bowl cream the butter and sugar together for 15 minutes. Add the eggs, one at a time, beating after each addition just enough to blend.

In a bowl or on a sheet of waxed paper, sift together the flour and baking powder.

Add the flour to the creamed mixture alternately with the cream. Continue mixing until well blended. Add the almond and vanilla extracts. Stir well. Fold in the coconut and combine well. Pour the batter into the pan.

Place the pan in a cold oven and set the temperature to 300°. Bake 1¾ hours, or until a cake tester inserted into the center of the cake comes out clean.

Remove the cake to a cooling rack. Cool in the pan for 10 minutes. Turn the cake out onto the rack and continue cooling.

makes 1 cake

🌿 Pecan Cake

3¾ cups flour
1 teaspoon baking powder
4 teaspoons grated nutmeg
4 cups chopped pecans
5 cups golden raisins
1 cup dark raisins
½ pound softened butter
2 cups sugar
6 eggs
½ cup brandy

Preheat the oven to 275°. Butter a 10-inch tube pan and set aside.

In a large bowl stir together the flour, baking powder and nutmeg.

Remove ½ cup of the flour mixture and add it to the pecans and raisins in a separate bowl. Mix and set aside.

Cream the butter and sugar until light and fluffy. Add the eggs, 2 at a time. Beat thoroughly after each addition.

Add the flour mixture to the creamed butter alternately with the brandy. Mix after each addition until well blended. Add the pecan-raisin mixture and mix thoroughly.

Turn the batter into the tube pan. Bake in the center of the oven for 2 hours.

Remove to a cooling rack. Cool in the pan for 15 minutes. Turn the cake out and cool completely on a rack.

makes 1 10-inch cake

🌿 Old-Fashioned Walnut Molasses Bars

¼ cup boiling water
¼ cup butter
¼ cup lard
½ cup brown sugar
½ cup molasses
1 teaspoon baking soda
3 cups flour
1 teaspoon salt
½ tablespoon ground ginger
⅓ teaspoon grated nutmeg
1 cup or more chopped walnuts

Preheat the oven to 350°. Grease two baking sheets and set them aside.

Place the butter and lard in a large bowl. Pour the boiling water over them. Add the sugar, molasses, baking soda, flour, salt, ginger and nutmeg. Mix until well blended. Place the dough in the refrigerator and chill for 2 to 3 hours.

Roll the dough out on a lightly floured surface to ¼-inch thickness. With a pastry wheel or sharp knife, cut the dough into strips 3½ × 1½ inches. Sprinkle the strips with the chopped walnuts and carefully place them on the baking sheets.

Bake for 10 minutes or until done. Cool completely on racks.

makes approximately 50 to 60 bars

Key Lime Pie

1 cup plus 2 tablespoons sugar
⅓ cup cornstarch
¼ cup cold water
½ teaspoon salt
1½ cups hot water
6 tablespoons lime juice
3 eggs, separated
3 tablespoons butter
1 tablespoon grated lime rind
1 9-inch pastry shell
6 tablespoons sugar
⅛ teaspoon salt
1 sliced lime, for garnish

Preheat the oven to 450°.

Roll out the pastry on a lightly floured surface. Fit it into a 9-inch pie plate. Prick the shell all over with a fork and bake for 12 to 15 minutes. Cool completely. Reduce the oven temperature to 300°.

In a saucepan combine the 1 cup plus 2 tablespoons sugar, the cornstarch, ½ teaspoon salt, and cold water. Mix well. Add the hot water and cook over very low heat, stirring constantly, until the mixture is very thick. Remove the saucepan from the heat and stir in the lime juice. Return the saucepan to low heat and cook until the mixture is thickened.

In a small bowl lightly beat the egg yolks. Beat in 1 teaspoon of the sugar mixture in the saucepan.

Remove the saucepan from the heat and slowly stir in the egg yolks. Return the saucepan to the heat and cook for 2 minutes, stirring constantly. Add the butter and the grated lime rind. Stir well. Remove the saucepan from the heat and cool.

Pour the cooled filling into the pie shell.

In a small bowl beat the egg whites until they are stiff but not dry. Gradually beat in the 6 tablespoons sugar and the ⅛ teaspoon salt. Beat until well blended.

Spread the meringue over the top of the pie and bake for 20 minutes. Cool before serving.

serves 6 to 8

Pecan Pie

4 eggs
2 cups dark corn syrup
2 tablespoons butter, melted and cooled
1 teaspoon pure vanilla extract
1 9-inch pastry shell
1½ cups pecan halves

Preheat the oven to 400°.

On a lightly floured board roll out the pastry. Fit it into a 9-inch pie plate. Line the pastry with a buttered sheet of aluminum foil pressed gently into the shell. Bake the pastry for 10 minutes. Remove the foil and bake for 2 minutes longer. Remove the pie shell from the oven and cool.

In a large bowl, whisk the eggs for about 30 seconds or until smooth. Continue whisking and pour in the corn syrup in a slow continuous stream. Add the vanilla and melted butter. Continue to whisk until the ingredients are well blended.

Pour the mixture into the cooled pie shell. Top it with the pecan halves.

Bake on the middle shelf of the oven for 35 to 40 minutes or until firm. Serve warm with whipped cream.

serves 8

❧ Rhubarb Pie

2 cups cut-up rhubarb
1½ cups sugar
½ teaspoon salt
1½ tablespoons cornstarch
1 egg, beaten
2 tablespoons butter
2 pastries for 9-inch pies

Preheat the oven to 425°.

Cut the rhubarb into 1-inch pieces. Do not peel the pieces. Place the pieces in a bowl and cover with boiling water for 1 minute. Drain and reserve.

Combine the sugar, salt, and cornstarch together in a mixing bowl. Add the egg and the rhubarb.

Fit one of the pastries into a 9-inch pie pan. Fit well and crimp. Fill the shell with the rhubarb mixture and dot with butter.

Cut strips of dough with a sharp knife or pastry wheel from the second pastry. Make a lattice across the top of the pie pan and crimp the edges.

Bake for 35 to 40 minutes, or until the rhubarb is tender. Cool before serving.

serves 8

❧ Flan

¼ cup sugar
½ cup sugar
3 eggs
3 cups milk
½ teaspoon pure vanilla extract

Preheat the oven to 350°.

In a saucepan heat ¼ cup sugar until it becomes a light brown syrup. Coat the sides and bottom of a custard dish or medium soufflé dish with the syrup. Set aside to cool.

In a mixing bowl beat the eggs and ½ cup sugar. Add the milk and vanilla. Beat well.

Pour the mixture into the coated custard dish. Set the dish into a pan of hot water and bake for 30 minutes, or until a knife inserted into the center comes out clean.

serves 4

❧ Brown Sugar Pie

1 cup firmly packed brown sugar
1 egg, slightly beaten
2 tablespoons flour
3 tablespoons milk
1 teaspoon pure vanilla extract
2 tablespoons melted butter
1 pastry for 9-inch pie

Preheat the oven to 350°.

Roll the pie pastry out onto a lightly floured surface. Fit it into pie shell and flute edges. Set aside.

In a large bowl combine the brown sugar, egg, flour, milk, vanilla extract and melted butter. Mix until well blended.

Pour the mixture into the pie shell. Bake for 15 minutes or until set. Remove from the oven and let cool. Serve warm.

serves 6 to 8

🌿 Osgood Pie

½ cup butter
1 cup sugar
2 eggs, separated
½ cup chopped pecans
½ cup raisins
½ teaspoon ground cloves
½ teaspoon cinnamon
2 teaspoons cocoa
1 teaspoon vinegar
1 pastry for 9-inch pie

Preheat the oven to 375°.

Roll the pastry out onto a lightly floured surface. Fit it into a 9-inch pie plate and flute the edges. Set aside.

In a large bowl cream the butter and sugar together until they are light and fluffy. Beat the egg yolks and add them to the creamed mixture. Blend well.

Stir in the pecans, raisins, cloves, cinnamon cocoa and vinegar. Mix well.

In a small bowl, beat the egg whites until they are stiff but not dry. Fold the egg whites into the sugar mixture.

Turn the mixture into the pie shell and bake for 10 minutes. Reduce the heat to 325° and bake for 30 minutes longer. Cool before serving.

serves 6 to 8

🌿 Kentucky Bourbon Cake

1½ cups softened butter
2 cups sugar
2¼ cups firmly packed light brown sugar
6 eggs
5½ cups flour
¼ teaspoon salt
1 teaspoon grated nutmeg
2 cups Bourbon whiskey
3½ cups coarsely chopped pecans

Preheat the oven to 300°. Heavily grease a 10-inch tube pan. Flour lightly and shake out excess. Set aside.

In a very large mixing bowl cream the butter until soft.

In a medium-sized bowl combine the sugar and brown sugar. Mix well. Add half the sugar mixture to the butter and cream until it is very smooth.

In another bowl beat the eggs until they are light and fluffy. Slowly beat in the remaining sugar mixture. Continue beating until the mixture is smooth and creamy. Add to the butter mixture and stir until thoroughly combined.

Sift the flour, salt and nutmeg together. Add the flour and Bourbon alternately to the batter, beginning and ending with the flour. Mix thoroughly. Stir in the pecan pieces.

Turn the batter into the tube pan and bake for 1½ to 1¾ hours or until the cake begins to shrink from the pan.

Remove the cake from the oven and cool in the pan for 15 minutes. Turn out onto rack and cool completely. This cake improves with age. Wrap it tightly in aluminum foil and store for a week before serving.

makes 1 10-inch cake

🌿 Condiments 🌿

In my grandma's day, when the ice in the icebox didn't last long in the heat of a Southern summer, pickles, relishes, preserves and other condiments were the only way to preserve the bounty of the summer harvest. She made her preserves and such just the way *her* grandma did. Well, now we have refrigerators and deep-freezes, of course, but we Southern cooks still cherish those old recipes. I still make my own preserves, just like my great-great-grandma did. Store-bought condiments just aren't the same.

Some of my old family favorites, like Lime Relish, may make your lips pucker, but tart condiments are the perfect accompaniment to rich roasts. Real, homemade Mint Relish leaves any other kind way behind. And it wouldn't be real Jam Cake if it were made with anything but homemade Old-Fashioned Blackberry Jam.

There's one other real nice thing about making your own condiments. They're a wonderful gift from your kitchen to your friends and family—and they'll think of you every time they open the jar and enjoy its contents.

🌿 Brandied Whole Peaches

4 pounds sugar
4 pounds ripe, unblemished whole peaches
2 cups brandy

In a large pot place the sugar and add enough water to dissolve. Bring the mixture to a boil. Add the peaches and cook for 5 minutes.

Remove the peaches and boil the syrup 15 minutes longer. Stir in the brandy. Remove the pot from the heat.

Place the peaches into six 1-pint sterilized jars. Pour the syrup over them. Seal, cool, and store.

makes approximately 6 pints

🌿 Country Tomato Preserves

5 pounds firm ripe tomatoes
5 pounds sugar
1 lemon, thinly sliced
1 small piece ginger root or 1 teaspoon ground
  ginger

Peel and chop the tomatoes. Place them in a large heavy pot and add the sugar, lemon and ginger. Stir well.

Bring the mixture to a boil. Reduce the heat and simmer slowly until the mixture is thick, about 45 minutes. Stir frequently. Remove the ginger root.

Carefully spoon the preserves into hot sterilized jars. Seal, cool, and store.

yields 24 ounces

🌿 Lime Relish

12 limes, washed
cold water
1½ cups sugar
1 cup vinegar
½ cup water

Place the limes in a large pot and add
enough cold water to cover. Soak the limes
for 24 hours.

Drain the limes and return them to the pot.
Add enough cold water to cover and cook
for 15 to 20 minutes, or until limes can be
easily pierced with a fork. Drain well and set
aside to cool.

When the limes are cool, cut them into
eighths. Remove the seeds. Set the limes
aside.

Place the sugar, vinegar and water in a
saucepan. Cook over medium-low heat until
syrupy, about 15 minutes.

Place the lime pieces into hot sterilized jars.
Cover with the syrup. Seal, cool, and store.

makes 2 pints

🌿 Mint Relish

½ cup fresh mint leaves
3 large tart apples, cored
1½ cups seedless raisins
12 firm ripe tomatoes
2 sweet red peppers, seeded
4 large onions
2 tablespoons mustard seeds
½ cup salt
2 cups sugar
6 cups cider vinegar

Coarsely chop the mint, apples, raisins,
tomatoes, red pepper and onions in a food
chopper, blender or food processor. Place the
mixture in a bowl. Stir in the mustard seeds,
salt, sugar and vinegar. Mix well.

Place the mixture into a crock or well-sealed
glass container for 10 days. Stir occasionally.

After 10 days, spoon the mixture into hot
sterilized jars. Seal, cool, and store.

🌿 Old-Fashioned Blackberry Jam

5 cups fresh ripe blackberries
½ cup water
4 cups sugar

Wash the berries and discard any unripe or
damaged fruit.

Place the berries into a heavy pot. Add the
water and sugar and bring to a boil. Stir
until the sugar dissolves. Reduce the heat to
medium-low and cook, uncovered, until the
jam reaches 221° on a candy thermometer.
Stir occasionally.

Remove the pot from the heat. Skim the top
of the mixture. Carefully spoon the jam into
hot sterilized jars. Seal, cool, and store.

yields 5 cups

🌿 Peach and Raisin Preserves

12 firm ripe peaches
2 cups seedless white or black raisins
4½ oranges, peeled
¼ cup shredded orange peel
sugar
1 cup finely chopped walnuts

Cook the whole peaches in a large pot of boiling water for 1 minute. Drain and run the peaches under cold water briefly. Remove the peach skins. Cut the peaches in half and remove the pits. Thinly slice the peaches and put them in a large bowl.

Finely grind the raisins in a food processor or blender. Add the raisins to the peaches.

Break the oranges into sections. Thinly slice and chop the sections. Add the oranges to the peaches and mix.

Measure out cupfuls of the peach mixture into a large saucepan. Add 1 cup of sugar for each cupful of peach mixture. Simmer the mixture over low heat for 30 minutes, stirring frequently, or until it is very thick.

Add the chopped walnuts and cook for 5 to 10 more minutes. Pour the preserves into hot sterilized 1-pint jars. Seal, cool and store.

makes 4 pints

🌿 Plum Butter

3 pounds fresh purple plums
3 cups honey
3 ounces lemon juice
3 ounces orange juice
grated rind of ½ lemon

Wash the plums and remove the stems. Halve and pit the plums.

Put the halved plums in a large saucepan and add enough cold water to half-cover the plums. Cover the saucepan and cook over medium heat for 10 to 15 minutes, or until the plums are very soft. Remove the saucepan from the heat and cool for 5 minutes. Purée the plums in a blender or food processor.

Pour the puréed plums back into the saucepan and add the honey, lemon juice, orange juice and lemon rind. Simmer, uncovered over low heat for about 3 hours, or until the mixture is very dark and thick.

Pour the plum butter into hot sterilized 1-pint jars. Seal, cool, and store.

makes 2n pints

❧ Southern Mixed Chutney

1 quart white vinegar
1 pound ripe mangoes, peeled and sliced
3 pounds apples, peeled, cored, and sliced
1 pound dark brown sugar
1 ounce fresh chili peppers, finely chopped
1 cup seedless golden raisins
½ pound finely cut dried lemon peel
½ pound candied ginger, chopped
2 garlic cloves, crushed
2 ounces mustard seeds
2 teaspoons salt
2 teaspoons confectioner's sugar

In a large pot bring the vinegar to a boil. Add the mangoes and apples. Cook until soft, about 20 to 25 minutes.

Add the brown sugar, chili pepper, raisins, lemon peel, ginger and garlic. Add the mustard seeds, salt and sugar. Mix well and cook for 15 minutes.

Remove the saucepan from the heat and pour the chutney into hot sterilized jars. Seal, cool, and store.

makes approximately 3 quarts

❧ Southern-Style Green Tomato Relish

4 to 5 pounds green tomatoes, chopped
2 medium-sized onions, chopped
2 quarts cold water
½ cup salt
1½ cups white vinegar
½ cup boiling water
1½ cups sugar
1½ teaspoons celery seeds
½ teaspoon cinnamon
½ teaspoon ground turmeric
¼ teaspoon dry mustard

Place the tomatoes and onions in a large bowl. Pour the cold water over them and sprinkle with the salt. Soak for 3 hours.

Drain the tomatoes and onions in a colander. Rinse well with cold water.

In a saucepan combine the vinegar, boiling water, sugar, celery seeds, cinnamon, turmeric and mustard. Bring the mixture to a boil and boil for 3 minutes. Add the tomatoes and onions and bring to a boil again. Lower the heat and simmer again, uncovered, for 10 minutes. Remove from heat.

Carefully spoon the relish into hot sterilized jars. Seal, cool, and store.

makes approximately 2 to 2½ pints

❧ Chili Sauce

4 cups water
1 teaspoon salt
½ cup chili powder
3 tablespoons lard
1 garlic clove, crushed

Bring the water and the salt to a boil in a saucepan.

In a small bowl combine the chili powder and just enough cold water to make a paste. Add this to the boiling water along with the lard. Stir well.

Reduce the heat and simmer for 15 to 20 minutes or until the mixture has the consistency of tomato sauce. Stir in the garlic.

For a hotter or thicker sauce, add more chili powder. Store tightly covered in the refrigerator.

makes approximately 3 cups

🌿 Green Chili Sauce

3 fresh or canned green chili peppers, with seeds, chopped
4 medium-sized green tomatoes, chopped
2 medium-sized onions, chopped
1 cup boiling water
1 garlic clove, finely chopped
1 teaspoon dried oregano
salt to taste

Place the chopped chilies in a saucepan. Add enough water to cover and bring to a boil. Cook the chilies for 10 minutes. Remove from the heat and drain well.

Return the chilies to the saucepan and add the tomatoes, onions and boiling water. Simmer over medium heat for 20 minutes.

Remove from the heat and press the mixture through a sieve. Discard any solids remaining in the sieve. Add the garlic, oregano and salt. Stir well. The mixture should be very thick.

Store tightly covered in the refrigerator.

makes approximately 2 cups

🌿 Mango Chutney

4 pounds semiripe mangos
3 cups cider vinegar
2 cups dark brown sugar
2 cups seedless raisins
1 cup currants
2 cups finely chopped onions
4 large garlic cloves, crushed
1 3-inch piece fresh ginger root, very thinly sliced
1 teaspoon ground cloves

Peel the mangos, remove the pits, and cut the mangoes into 1½-inch chunks.

In a large, 8-quart pot place the mangos, vinegar, sugar, raisins, currants, onions, garlic, ginger and cloves. Bring to a boil over high heat. Stir until the sugar dissolves. Reduce the heat to low and simmer, uncovered, for 20 to 25 minutes. Stir occasionally. Remove from the heat when the mango pieces are tender but still intact.

Spoon the chutney carefully into hot sterilized jars. Seal, cool, and store.

makes 3 quarts

🌿 Peach Chutney

4 quarts peaches, chopped
1 cup chopped onion
1 garlic clove, chopped
1 hot red pepper pod
1 cup raisins
1 quart vinegar
2 tablespoons ground ginger
¼ cup mustard seeds
3 cups brown sugar
2 teaspoons salt

Place the chopped peaches into a large pot. Add the onion, raisins, vinegar, brown sugar and salt. Mix well.

Combine the garlic, hot pepper, ginger and mustard seeds. Place them into a square of doubled cheesecloth and tie it closed with string.

Bring the peach mixture to a boil. When mixture begins to boil, add the bag with the spices. Reduce the heat and cook, stirring frequently, until thick, about 40 minutes.

Remove the spice bag. Pour the peach mixture into hot sterilized jars. Seal, cool, and store.

makes 4 pints

🌿 Pickled Peaches

12 peaches (about 3 pounds)
12 whole cloves
4½ cups sugar
water
3 cups cider vinegar
4 cinnamon sticks, coarsely broken

In a large pot boil enough water to cover the peaches. When the water boils, add the peaches, four at a time, and let boil for 2 to 3 minutes. Drain the peaches and rinse them with cold water.

Peel the peaches with a sharp knife. Stick a clove into each peach and put them into large sterilized jars.

Place the sugar, vinegar and cinnamon in a large saucepan. Bring the mixture to a boil. Stir only until the sugar dissolves. Remove from the heat and carefully spoon the syrup over the peaches, a little at a time. Allow the syrup to settle before adding more.

Cover the jars tightly and cool to room temperature. Refrigerate for 4 or more days before serving.

makes 2 quarts

🌿 Pickled Figs

1 gallon water
1 tablespoon baking soda
6 pounds fresh figs, stemmed and washed
3 pounds sugar
2 cups white wine vinegar
1 tablespoon cinnamon
1½ teaspoons whole cloves
2 lemons, thinly sliced

Bring the water to a boil in a large pot. Add the baking soda and dissolve. Remove from the heat. Add the figs and let them soak for 10 minutes.

Drain the figs and rinse them in cold water.

In another pot place the sugar, vinegar, cinnamon, cloves and lemons. Add the figs and bring the mixture to a boil. Cook until the liquid is clear.

Remove the figs and place them in sterilized jars. Boil the syrup until it thickens. Pour the syrup over the figs. Seal the jars, cool, and store.

makes 8 pints

🌿 Citrus Conserve

6 oranges
5 cups water
6 cups sugar
¼ cup fresh lime juice
1 2-inch cinnamon stick
½ cup seedless raisins

Wash and quarter the oranges. Remove the peel. Cut the pulp finely, discarding the membranes and seeds.

Chop the peel finely in a food chopper, blender or food processor. Place the peel in a saucepan, cover it with the water and bring to a boil. Reduce the heat to medium and cook until the peel is tender, about 20 minutes. Add the orange pulp and juice and cook 20 minutes longer, or until the mixture has cooked down to half its original volume.

Add the sugar, lime juice, cinnamon and raisins. Cook, stirring constantly, until the sugar is totally dissolved, about 30 minutes.

Remove from the heat. Carefully spoon the mixture into hot sterilized jars. Seal, cool, and store.

makes approximately 3 pints

❧ Meal Planners ❧

Weekday Dinner I

Charleston Crab Cakes (page 7)
Plantation Chicken and Vegetable Stew
   (page 71)
Squash and Corn Pudding (page 83)
Southern Rum Pie (page 113)
Saffron Bread (page 99)

Weekday Dinner II

Herbed Bean Salad (page 25)
Chicken Fried Steak with Spicy Gravy (page
   29)
Smothered Parsnips (page 79)
Carolina Rick Pilau (page 81)
Jam Cake with Fruit Frosting (page 108)

Hearty Weekday Dinner

Mulligatawny Soup (page 21)
Shrimp Creole (page 56)
Minted Carrots (page 74)
Red Rice (page 81)
Buttermilk Biscuits (page 95)
Charleston Torte (page 105)

Country Dinner

Beefy Okra Soup (page 21)
Country-Style Ham (page 34)
Down-Home Carrot Casserole (page 75)
Manor House Apple Salad (page 25)
Osgood Pie (page 118)

Fried Chicken Dinner

Spicy Chick Pea Salad (page 26)
Southern Fried Chicken (page 49)
Grits and Cheese Casserole (page 78)
Colonial Cherry Pudding (page 106)
Cornsticks (page 96)

Sunday Dinner I

Latin Quarter Green Tomatoes (page 10)
Jambalaya (page 46)
Brandied Sweet Potatoes (page 84)
Pecan Pie (page 116)
Corn Bread (page 96)

Sunday Dinner II

Corn and Shrimp Chowder (page 14)
Orange Grove Pork Chops (page 33)
Stuffed Acorn Squash (page 82)
Country Green Beans (page 77)
Charlotte Russe (page 105)

New Year's Dinner I

Shreveport Shrimp (page 10)
Stuffed Lettuce Heads (page 24)
Gumbo Filé (page 72)
Hoppin' John (page 74)
Sweet Potato Rolls (page 100)
Pecan Butter Balls (page 113)

New Year's Dinner II

Hambone Soup (page 14)
Fried Oysters (page 52)
Southern-Style Potato Salad (page 26)
New Year's Blackeyed Peas (page 76)
Kentucky Bourbon Cake (page 109)

Party Dinner

Avocado Appetizer (page 7)
Mardi Gras Seafood Gumbo (page 72)
Sweet Potato Pone (page 85)
Benne Biscuits (page 93)
Key Lime Pie (page 116)

Index